Also by Louis Jenkins

European Shoes

North of the Cities

Sea Smoke

The Winter Road

Just Above Water

Nice Fish

All Tangled Up with the Living

An Almost Human Gesture

Before You Know It

Before You Know It

PROSE POEMS 1970–2005

Louis Jenkins

Will o' the Wisp Books
Duluth, Minnesota

Published by Will o' the Wisp Books 2009

Printed in Canada

Cover painting by Ann Jenkins

Cover design by Amy Jenkins

ISBN 978-0-9793128-2-3

Versions of some of these poems originally appeared in the following publications: Agni, American Poetry Review, Ascent, Barnwood, Black Warrior Review, Borealis, Boston Review, Caprice, Carleton Miscellany, Chariton Review, Cimarron Review, Coda, Columbia, Crazy Horse, Epoch, Everywhere, Gettysburg Review, Great River Review, Hawaii Review, Ironwood, Jublilat, Kenyon Review, Key Satch(el), Knockout, Lake Country Journal, Lake Superior Journal, Lamp In The Spine, Literary Cavalcade, Luna, Manhattan Review, Midwest Quarterly, Milkweed Chronicle, Minnesota English Journal, Ninth Letter, Paragraph, Paris Review, Paterson Literary Review, Poetry Daily, Poetry East, Poetry International, Poetry Now, The Prose Poem: An International Journal, Puerto Del Sol, Parabola, Redactions, Red Weather, Rosebud, Seneca Review, Sentence, Snowy Egret, Speakeasy, Tarpaulin Sky. Terminus, The Sun, Three Candles, Utne, Virginia Quarterly Review, Willow Springs.

Will o' the Wisp Books
101 Clover Street
Duluth, Minnesota
55812-1103
www.willothewispbooks.com

TABLE OF CONTENTS

1988–1995

1996–2000

TO THE READER

The prose poems in this selection were written between 1970 and 2005, but some have been revised within the last two years. Some were changed only slightly, while others, I felt, needed more extensive work. All the changes seemed necessary to me and seemed to bring the poems closer to my original intent. You, the reader, might not agree with my changes, but since some of these poems were written long ago, chances are good that you never read the first versions, or if you did, you have, no doubt, forgotten them by now.
                -Louis Jenkins

FORWARD BY MARK RYLANCE

Sometimes a man who has recently had a haircut asks me, "What is the use of poetry?". I get distracted by his hair line and lack of ear hair and wonder how much a man pays for a good haircut in this city or whether those electric nose hair cutters are really worth it during this economic downturn.

When I look the man in the eyes again, I see he is sneaking a peak at my receding hairline and already, in his head, adding another utility hook to that tool shed or concrete basement den. He's thinking, "Time to get me one of those..." I'm not a good enough mind reader to catch the name, but I can see it's some kind of machine that spins a piece of nylon fishing wire so fast it will cut down everything that grows where your lawnmower can't mow.

Other questions: "What are you thinking about?", "Where's the nearest bicycle shop?", "Who's your favourite...?" also befuddle me. I have tried to prepare myself for "Who's you favourite?", as I sometimes have to be interviewed on the radio or television to sell the particular show I am in. I am an actor. When the dreadful question is asked, I still don't know what to say. There seem to be so many answers. Invariably, I have to make something up. Regret and recriminations follow at internal boardroom meetings. Some time ago, I was nominated to attend a couple of award ceremonies in New York City. I had been before and knew the territory to be a relative minefield.

The Tony Awards take place in Radio City music hall. The hall holds something like 5000 people, maybe 8000, and a million more, they say, are watching at home. Every few minutes, there's a break so that the people at home can be relieved of their confusion about what they need in their life. This only takes a few minutes, but the whole event lasts longer than an uncut Shakespeare tragedy, and there is no interval, so people have to go to the rest room. This is not a problem though because as soon as the break occurs, a small, rather depressed line of well-dressed people with very good haircuts, walk around the aisles behind a woman with headphones who directs them to sit in any seat that has been vacated. This way the event is never ruined by the lack of a full house.

I know this, because against my better instincts I too was sitting there amongst the 1,005,000 people, watching as Private Ryan after Private Ryan was called up in front of us to rush through, sometimes in tears, a list of other people who were also to blame for what they were accused of having done. All this to the accompaniment of loud music and in front of a growing crowd of disappointed nominees and supporters, some of whom have paid hundreds of dollars, or just realized they will lose thousands of dollars, or wonder whether a million dollars would be enough to convince them to attend something like this again! Why hadn't I listened to George C. Scott? Marlon Brando? Duchamp? Brunel? Walt or the beloved Jellalludin Rumi? What the hell was I doing with my life? Who had I become?

"What is the use of poetry?", especially the poetry of my beloved Mr. Louis Jenkins? If you Google mark rylance tony award speech, you will find one. I use poetry all the time. I eat Mr. Jenkins' poetry like bread; like a tortoise eats greens and you know he's ill when he don't. Jenkins is a necessity of survival to any tortoise on this hare brained grand prix derby day winner takes all racetrack of these, our sunset glory dinosaur days.
 -Mark Rylance

1970–1987

WALKING THROUGH A WALL

Unlike flying or astral projection, walking through walls is a totally earth-related craft, but a lot more interesting than pot making or driftwood lamps. I got started at a picnic up in Bowstring in the northern part of the state. A fellow walked through a brick wall right there in the park. I said, "Say, I want to try that." Stone walls are best, then brick and wood. Wooden walls with fiberglass insulation and steel doors aren't so good. They won't hurt you. If your wall walking is done properly, both you and the wall are left intact. It is just that they aren't pleasant somehow. The worst things are wire fences. Maybe it's the molecular structure of the alloy or just the amount of give in a fence, I don't know, but I've torn my jacket and lost my hat in a lot of fences. The best approach to a wall is, first, two hands placed flat against the surface; it's a matter of concentration and just the right pressure. You will feel the dry, cool inner wall with your fingers. Then there is a moment of total darkness before you step through on the other side.

VIOLENCE ON TELEVISION

It is best to turn on the set only after all the stations have gone off the air and just watch the snowfall. This is the other life you have been promising yourself; somewhere back in the woods, ten miles from the nearest town, and that just a wide place in the road with a tavern and a gas station. When you drive home, after midnight, half drunk, the roads are treacherous. And your wife is home alone, worried, looking anxiously out at the snow. This snow has been falling steadily for days, so steadily the snowplows can't keep up. So you drive slowly, peering down the road. And there! Did you see it? Just at the edge of your headlight beams, something, a large animal, or a man, crossed the road. Stop. There he is among the birches, a tall man wearing a white suit. No, it isn't a man. Whatever it is it motions to you, an almost human gesture, then retreats farther into the woods. He stops and motions again. The snow is piling up all around the car. Are you coming?

CONFESSIONAL POEM

I have this large tattoo on my chest. It is like a dream I have while I am awake. I see it in the mirror as I shave and brush my teeth, or when I change my shirt or make love. What can I do? I can't remember where I got the tattoo. When in the past did I live such a life? And the price of having such a large tattoo removed must be completely beyond reason. Still, the workmanship of the drawing is excellent, a landscape 8 x 10 inches in full color, showing cattle going downhill into a small western town. A young man, who might have been my great-grandfather, dressed as a cowboy and holding a rifle, stands at the top of the hill and points down toward the town. The caption beneath the picture reads: "Gosh, I didn't know we were this far west."

MOTORCYCLE

He climbs on, switches on the ignition, kicks the starter: once, twice, three, four, five times…. Nothing. He tries a dozen more times. It won't go. He checks the gas tank. Got gas. He switches the key off and on, tries again. It still won't go. He climbs off the bike and squats down to look at the engine. Check the carburetor, check the wires…seems okay. He takes a wrench from his jacket pocket and removes the spark plug. He examines it, blows on it, wipes it on his jeans, replaces the plug, climbs back on the bike and tries again. Nothing. Now he is getting really angry. There is absolutely no reason why this thing shouldn't start. He gets off the bike and stands and stares at it. He gets back on and kicks the starter really hard half-a-dozen times. Now he is furious. He gets off and throws the wrench he is still holding as far as he can. It bounces on the gravel down the road and skids into the weeds in the ditch. Then he turns and kicks the son-of-a-bitch motorcycle over on its side and walks away. After a short distance he thinks better of it and returns to the motorcycle. It isn't sobbing quietly. It doesn't say, "I don't want to play with you anymore," or "I don't love you anymore," or "I have my own life to live," or "I have the children to think of." It only lies there leaking oil and gas. He rights the motorcycle and carefully wipes off the dust, carefully mounts and once more tries the starter. Even now it won't go. He gets down and sits in the dirt beside the broken motorcycle.

APPOINTED ROUNDS

At first he refused to deliver junk mail because it was stupid, all those deodorant ads, moneymaking ideas and contests. Then he began to doubt the importance of the other mail he carried. He began to randomly select first-class mail for non-delivery. After he had finished his mail route each day he would return home with his handful of letters and put them in the attic. He didn't open them and never even looked at them again. It was as if he were an agent of Fate, capricious and blind. In the several years before he was caught, friends vanished, marriages failed, business deals fell through. Toward the end he became more and more bold, deleting houses, then whole blocks from his route. He began to feel he'd been born in the wrong era. If only he could have been a Pony Express rider galloping into some prairie town with an empty bag, or the runner from Marathon collapsing in the streets of Athens, gasping, "No news."

SKILLET

The skillet is heavy and black, too heavy to carry on a long hike, but completely functional. The skillet has lived a life of service, worked hard. The skillet will not accept charity.

The skillet's mouth is always open as if it were trying to tell me something of fire, of darkness and poverty but manages only to sputter platitudes of protestant virtue.

Still, I believe the skillet has some understanding of its life. For a few moments each morning when I fry eggs the skillet opens its large eyes and stares intently at me and at the fork in my hand.

THE PLAGIARIST

A fat teaching assistant has caught a freshman cheating on his exam and she stands now in the hallway displaying the evidence, telling the story to her colleagues: "I could tell by the way he looked. I could tell by his hands." With each detail the story expands, rooms are added, hallways, chandeliers, flights of stairs, and she sinks exhausted against a railing. More listeners arrive and she begins again. She seems thinner now, lighter. She rises, turns. She seems almost to be dancing. She clutches the paper of the wretched student. He holds her firmly, gently, as they turn and turn across the marble floor. The lords and ladies fall back to watch as they move toward the balcony and the summer night. Below in the courtyard soldiers assemble, their brass and steel shining in the moonlight.

LIBRARY

I sit down at a table and open a book of poems and move slowly into the shadow of tall trees. They are white pines, I think. The ground is covered with soft brown needles and there are signs that animals have come here silently and vanished before I could catch sight of them. But here the trail edges into a cedar swamp: wet ground, dead fall and rotting leaves. I move carefully but rapidly, pleased with myself. Someone else comes and sits down at the table, a serious looking young man with a large stack of books. He takes a book from the top of the stack and opens it. The book is called How to *Get a High-Paying Job*. He flips through it and lays it down and picks up another and pages through it quickly. It is titled *Moving Ahead*. We are moving ahead more rapidly now, through a second growth of popple and birch, our faces scratched and our clothes torn by the underbrush. We are moving even faster, marking the trail, followed closely by bulldozers and crews from the paper company.

MARLENE NOLUND

She's packed the kids off to spend the weekend with their father. At last she has the place to herself, a rented farmhouse, a couple dozen chickens, a pickup that works part-time and a child support check she finally managed to get from her ex-husband. His problem was that he didn't want anything much. He was happy being a bricklayer or being in the army, happy just hanging around the house. She puts on her best dress and stands in front of the mirror brushing her hair. She looks good, a little big in the chest maybe, but good for being the mother of two. It's mid-afternoon and the whole weekend is ahead. The summer wind nags at the house and flaps the blind at the window behind her so that it sounds like someone impatiently turning the pages of a newspaper. She imagines a man there, lying on the bed, glancing up occasionally to hurry her along, jingling the change in his pocket. It makes her nervous and angry. She fidgets with the dress, extracts a pair of earrings from the clutter of perfume and baby bottles on the bureau, smears her makeup. She hurries. It isn't what she wants.

A PHOTOGRAPH

She's been dead fifty years now. This photo was taken in 1902, just a girl, clowning for the camera. But when a baby is born in the family someone says, "See it has her eyes, her nose." And it's true. The argument continues. "I'm a farmer," I say, "a business man. I can't be wasting time in town, hanging out at the cafe, drinking coffee." It's spring and the roads are impassable. I stand in the barnyard, knee-deep in mud, dumbfounded, surrounded by insolent chickens. She says, "I never want to leave here." At night she whispers, "You have never loved me. You think only of yourself. You won't be allowed to enter the Promised Land." Then she giggles and pokes me in the ribs. "The children are asleep now," she says.

BREAD

Bread rising! The intoxicating smell of yeast. And bread fresh from the oven. Someone loves me and has left warm bread. When bread is broken, the life hidden within presents itself, a thousand little holes, windows open for the first time. In one booth near the window, four old women are drinking tea. They are dressed in old-fashioned clothes, layer on layer, suits and furs, jewelry handed down for generations. One woman names the year of her mother's birth, and another the day her husband died; his clothes still hang in the closet. They talk calmly, quietly, the spring sunlight coming through the glass to touch the backs of their hands…. Sit down. Share this bread. As we talk you can explain the ordinary things. I will play some music for you that isn't mine.

THE LIGHTHOUSE

Light flashes across the water and is gone, like headlights across the wall of a dark room where someone is lying awake. It happens so quickly, no way to take back the things that were said. Your son drove headlong into a train. Your daughter is in a Mexican jail. It's a house passed at eighty miles an hour. Did anyone live there? The night, the sea, the wind and the rocks, the terrible current off shore.... It is good to see the light across the water. It is a warning. This is the place where the land ends and the water begins or the water ends and the land begins. Either way is dangerous.

THE POET

He is young and thin with dark hair and a deep, serious voice. He sips his coffee and says, "I have found that it is a good idea to check the words you use in a dictionary. I keep a list. Here is the word *meadow*. Since I was a child the word meadow always had connotations of peace and beauty. Once I used meadow in a poem and as a matter of practice I looked the word up. I found that a meadow was a small piece of grassland used to graze animals… Somehow meadow was no longer a thing of beauty…."

It is spring. A few cows are grazing in the muddy meadow. There are patches of blackened snow beside the road. It is nearly dark and the ragged poplars at the far end of the meadow have turned black. The animals, the stones, the grass, everything near the earth darkens, and above: the *azure* sky.

FISHING BELOW THE DAM

On summer evenings the workingmen gather to fish in the swift water below the dam. They sit on the rocks and are silent for the most part, looking into the water and casting again and again. Lines tangle, tackle is lost and a fisherman curses to himself. No one notices. It is simply a part of the routine, like the backs of their wives in bed at night or short words to the children in the morning. Only the water holds their attention, crashing through the spillway with enough force behind it to break a man's back. And the undertow could take you as easily as a bit of fish line and toss you ashore miles downstream. The men shout to be heard above the roar of the water. ANY LUCK? NO I JUST GOT HERE.

FROST FLOWERS

In the morning people go off to work all wrapped and bundled, through frozen doors, over cracking snow, huffing and puffing, each fueled by some simmering private indignation: low pay, something that was said at break.... The sun is far away on the southern horizon, a vague hope, more distant than the Caribbean. Eight below zero at eleven o'clock. The coffee boils and grows bitter. All afternoon, the same old thing, knucklebone of mastodon stews on the stove. The radiator hisses at the long shadows that finally engulf the winter day. Lights come on for a time in the houses and go out one by one. We breathe deeply of the dark, we exhale great plumes and fronds that form on the windows, intricate icy blossoms open around us all night.

SERGEANT NORQUIST

Two years ago I thought seriously about killing myself. I looked at guns in the pawnshops. Then, I don't know why exactly, I turned to God. I have my job at the paper mill and this room, but they mean nothing to me. My real life begins when I put on this uniform and make my rounds. I go to all the bars downtown, even the worst ones along First Street. I say "Good evening, Salvation Army" and people give me their change, good people mostly. Once in a while a guy will say, "This ain't no church" or something like that, but no one has ever really given me a hard time. Most people respect the uniform. One evening in The Oasis a woman kissed me. I gave her a copy of the *War Cry*. She wasn't an old woman, either, but she had lived hard. I still pray for her. A lot of people talk to me. They tell me their days are hard to get through and I know about that. At night, sometimes, when I can't sleep, I think of all the money I've collected. I close my eyes and see all those nickels and dimes rising from the bars on First Street and from run-down places all over town, from poor people, like a reversed rain, from earth to heaven. I think nothing in heaven would grow if that rain didn't fall.

RESTAURANT OVERLOOKING
LAKE SUPERIOR

Late afternoon. Only a few old men at the bar, drinking and talking quietly. Waitresses for the evening shift begin to arrive. One stands for a moment at the far end of the dining room and looks out the window facing the lake. Snow is falling. The lake is completely obscured, still customers will ask for tables near the window. A few early diners begin to arrive, then others. Soon the room is filled with sounds—people talking, the rattle of dishes, the waitresses hurrying about. The lake is a great silence beneath all the noise. In their hurry the waitresses don't look out the window. Yet they are in her service, silent a moment as they fill the glasses with water.

LIFE IS SO COMPLEX

Life is so complex, even though you eat brown rice and brush your teeth with baking soda. Simplify. Spend the day alone. Spend it fishing. Watch the line and the motion of the water; your thoughts drift… a slight bump and a steady pull on the line and the whole line of cars begins to move as the train pulls out of the station. Someone takes the seat beside you, someone at the end of a love affair. The threats of murder and suicide, the pleading, the practical jokes, became at the end only tiresome and she is relieved at his going. She turns away before the train is out of sight.

Your ordinary life is simple, full of promise, bullet-like, pushing aside the waves of air, moving with incredible speed toward the life that waits, motionless, unsuspecting, at the heart of the forest.

A QUIET PLACE

I have come to understand my love for you. I came to you like a man, world-weary, looking for a quiet place. The gas station and grocery store, the church, the abandoned school, a few old houses, the river with its cool shady spots…. Good fishing. How I've longed for a place like this! As soon as I got here I knew I'd found it. Tomorrow the set production and camera crews arrive. We can begin filming on Monday: the story of a man looking for a quiet place.

THE BLIND MAN

He comes down the hill at a slight angle to the sidewalk, hesitantly, moving his red-tipped white cane from side to side until it touches the fender of a lavender Pontiac parked at the curb. Then he stops. He reaches out with his left hand until he touches the cold metal pole of a No Parking sign, pulls himself close, stands with his arm wrapped around the pole in the narrow space between pole and car, waits and listens. He seems unsure, seems to have difficulty sorting the various sounds. Traffic to the right, traffic behind, wind blowing uphill from the Lake, the sound of a few leaves on the concrete. No passersby. End of the day, end of fall. He listens, head slightly raised, hat pushed back, eyes closed. He is neither young nor old: a man between a car and a pole. He waits a long time. Then he moves his cane to the right, up into the rear wheelwell of the car, then away to the left. He releases the pole and takes two careful steps downhill, moving the cane in front of him.

SAILORS

When the ship gets into port the sailors all go nuts. They get drunk and dance and wake up the next afternoon in the whorehouse. And if a sailor gets thrown in jail he doesn't care because he just got paid and has enough money to get out. None of the sailors wants to go back to the ship. One thing sailors can't stand is the sight of water. One sailor hides out in a laundromat. One makes plans to marry. Another is still drunk. The sailors hate this lousy port. The ship sails at dawn with all hands, but someone has sneaked whiskey aboard. By midnight the crew is drunk and the ship is dead in the water. The captain is furious and shouts over the intercom to the engine room. But they are all asleep, rocked in their little cradle on the sea.

TWINS

The first baby they brought into my room was a girl. I held her for a few minutes then the nurse took her away. I never saw the baby again or the nurse that brought her. Later another nurse brought the boy, my son. When I told my husband he said it was probably just the effect of the anesthetic, but I made him check. They said there was only one baby born, a boy. I'm certain now there were two. I know the little girl is alive somewhere but I have no idea how to find her. I can only watch her brother for signs… you know, the way twins sense things about each other. Sometimes I'm afraid when he goes off to school, lost among so many other children. When he comes home in the afternoon I catch him and hold him a moment and look into his eyes before he pulls away to run outside and play with his friends. I can't really say what I'm looking for. I think I'll only know if something is missing, a certain look or a gesture…. I think I'll know if that life dies out in him. I can't explain that to him, of course, or to his father. He would only say I've got too much imagination.

THE UKRAINIAN EASTER EGG

It is quite different from the ordinary Ukrainian Easter Egg because of the pictures. On one side the sun is setting over Los Angeles and opposite, soldiers sitting in the muddy trenches. They look cold, smoking cigarettes. Here is the violin hidden in the soup kettle and there is a family of cats living in an abandoned gas station. There are so many pictures: the barbed wire and the road through the forest, the ducks, the radio, the smoky fires along the railroad track where the lovers are taking a walk. In the morning the elders of the village decide what must be done. A brave man must ride the fastest horse and deliver the egg. The journey is long, the roads are dangerous, the egg must be given only to the Czar.

FIRST SNOW

By dusk the snow is already partially melted. There are dark patches where the grass shows through, like islands in the sea seen from an airplane. Which one is home? The one I left as a child? They all seem the same now. What became of my parents? What about all those things I started and never finished? What were they? As we get older we become more alone. The man and his wife share this gift. It is their breakfast: coffee and silence, morning sunlight. They make love or they quarrel. They move through the day, she on the black squares, he on the white. At night they sit by fire, he reading his book, she knitting. The fire is agitated. The wind hoots in the chimney like a child blowing in a bottle, happily.

ASLEEP AT THE WHEEL

He falls asleep at the wheel and dreams that everything is the same; he is still driving at night through the long pine forest. Mile after mile glides through the automobile. He manages distances more easily now so there is time to discern in the night forest a single tree, a stone, or a hidden path. These things seem as familiar and absorbing as a love affair or his own childhood. He sees for the first time that the forest extends not fifty or a hundred miles, but infinitely on either side of the road, and that it is possible to wander there forever, alone, and not die... The car veers into the gravel at the edge of the blacktop. He wrenches the wheel back to the left. He is wide-awake. The car is on the road, speeding toward the end of its headlight beams.

MARGARET LUOMA

At her age a fall could have meant a serious injury, a sprained ankle or a broken hip. Luckily there was only a bruise and the terrible embarrassment. She pulled away from the young man who helped her to her feet, said "Thank you, I'm all right" and went on her way as quickly as she could without looking back. But she couldn't forget about it. His face… like a photograph on the piano, thoughtful, always young. "All that concern," she thought. "What did he care?" It began to seem as though he'd caused the bruises, actually pushed her down. She didn't need him. She was old now. A lifetime of love wasted.

THE DUTCH SHOE

She was out of the water for years, since the early fifties maybe, over at the shipyard in Superior. You could see her from the highway, her masts down, sails stowed away. I loved that boat. All the time I was growing up I made plans to buy her someday. What shall I say happened? That my father bought her and put her in the back yard and kept garden tools in the hold? Or that my mother bought her and kept her in the china closet with the jade Buddha and the eight-day clock? That her brass gleams in the firelight, still dry and harmless? No. I bought the Dutch Shoe and sailed to Rangoon and Singapore and a hundred other places. I faced incredible dangers and hardships. I talk loud and drink all night. When I snore I wake bears in the forest and fish in the sea. Early mist rises from the water. Ice forms on the masts. My hair has turned white and my teeth have fallen out. I can't see a thing and I am sailing away.

IN A TAVERN

"It's no use," he says, "she's left me." This is after several drinks. It's as if he had said, "Van Gogh is my favorite painter." It's a cheap print he has added to his collection. He's been waiting all evening to show it to me. He doesn't see it. To him it's an incredible landscape, empty, a desert. "My life is empty." He likes the simplicity. "My life is empty. She won't come back." It is a landmark, like the blue mountains in the distance that never change. The crust of sand gives way with each step, tiny lizards skitter out of the way.... Even after walking all day there is no change in the horizon. "We're lost," he says. "No," I say, "let's go on." He says, "You go on. Take my canteen. You've got a reason to live." "No," I say, "we're in this together and we'll both make it out of here."

A NEW CAR

He comes in late Saturday night, drunk. She pretends to be asleep when he comes to bed. Long before he wakes, Sunday morning, she is up and dressed. She dresses the child and drives away into the early fog. She drives 80 mph. over the blacktop country roads for several hours. When he wakes the sun is shining and the house is quiet. He has a hangover and thinks perhaps he has been robbed. He feels his pants pocket for his wallet. He stands at the window and looks out at the empty driveway. When she returns he is sitting at the kitchen table drinking coffee. "Where have you been?" he says. She says, "I had to take the baby to Sunday school, I can't depend on you to do it." He returns to the window and looks at the car. It's getting worn out he thinks, needs brakes and tires. He wishes he could afford a new one.

FOOTBALL

I take the snap from center, fake to the right, fade back, I've got protection. I've got a receiver open downfield…. What the hell is this? This isn't a football it's a shoe, a man's brown leather oxford. A cousin to a football maybe, the same skin, but not the same, a thing made for the earth, not the air. I realize that this is a world where anything is possible and I understand, also, that one often has to make do with what one has. I have eaten pancakes, for instance, with that clear corn syrup on them because there was no maple syrup and they weren't very good. Well, anyway, this is different. (My man downfield is waving his arms.) One has certain responsibilities, one has to make choices. This isn't right and I'm not going to throw it.

BASKETBALL

A huge summer afternoon with no sign of rain.... Elm trees in the farmyard bend and creak in the wind. The leaves are dry and gray. In the driveway a boy shoots a basketball at a goal above the garage door. Wind makes shooting difficult and time after time he chases the loose ball. He shoots, rebounds, turns, shoots...on into the afternoon. In the silence between the gusts of wind the only sounds are the thump of the ball on the ground and the rattle of the bare steel rim of the goal. The gate bangs in the wind, the dog in the yard yawns, stretches and goes back to sleep. A film of dust covers the water in the trough. Great clouds of dust rise from open fields that stretch a thousand miles beyond the horizon.

INTERMISSION

The violins have gone; the brass and woodwinds have gone. The orchestra has just finished a Paganini concerto. The basses and cellos lie on the floor or recline against chairs weary and unimpressed. They are like soldiers or prisoners on a ten-minute break and no one has any cigarettes. In a far corner, dressed in black, the drummer hunches over the tympani like a raven picking over a rabbit killed on the highway or like an old woman bending over a kettle brewing a poison to be painted on telephone poles to kill all the woodpeckers. He tunes and tests the drum. He puts his ear close. What does he hear? A distant storm? A herd of buffalo? Perhaps railroad crews working hard to lay down track a few miles ahead of a locomotive, the cars richly furnished with carpet, crystal and fine wine. The beautiful ladies and gentlemen come laughing and talking down the aisles to find their seats.

32 DEGREES F

The thermometer says exactly 32 degrees, freezing or melting. Neither here nor there…at the border, in a room without enough chairs, waiting with your bundle of possessions and the uneasy feeling that none of these things will be adequate on the other side. Outside the window a single drop of water hangs on the tip of an icicle for hours. A long time ago she showed me how to take the blossom at the base, snap off the stem, then carefully withdraw the pistil, pulling it slowly down until the little globe of nectar poised there, ready to take on the tongue. The single drop distilled from a lifetime falls to shatter on the frozen ground and the mindless soul flies away to its heaven on the honeysuckle south wind that's come five hundred miles over the snow.

THE FLOOD

Every so often, a girl calls me on the phone and tells me that she loves me, can't live without me, etc. The first time she called I was intrigued and flattered, naturally. But when I asked her name she ignored me and went right on talking. "Could we meet somewhere?" Again she ignored the question. Finally I became irritated and hung up. Obviously it was some kind of joke. She called several more times over the next few months and each time the result was the same. "What's the point?" I ask. "I love you," she says. A few weeks ago the bridge on 21st Street washed out. People came from all over town to help with the work and to watch the river overflow its banks and pour through the streets, the first flood in many years. Men were hard at work piling up sandbags to hold back the water. Near where I was standing, a pay telephone kept ringing and ringing. Finally, since no one else did, I answered. I thought perhaps it was someone calling with instructions for the flood control workers, but no. It was a man having trouble with his refrigerator. I guess he thought I was a repairman. No sooner had he hung up than the phone rang again: a woman looking for her child. No, I hadn't seen him. Call after call came in. It was as if people were actually telephoning the flood. For some reason I kept answering the phone. Then she called. "Hello," a pause. "Hello," I said again. "Ron," she said, "Ron, is that you?" I hung up the phone and stepped out of the booth. It was a relief to be in the open air again. I stood a moment looking at the muddy water while the phone continued to ring.

APPLEJACK

Wilma worked sixteen years for a plumbing and heating company and never married. She lived with her mother in a little house out in Arnold Township. And her mother, who was crazy from drinking applejack, would hide behind the door when Wilma came home from work and try to stab her with a butcher knife. Wilma didn't know what to do. When she thought of having her put in a rest home, the old lady would cry and Wilma's aunt in Seattle would write letters saying, "Don't you dare put my sister in a rest home." This went on for years and Wilma began drinking applejack too. When the old woman finally died, Wilma quit her job, lived alone in the house and wore her mother's clothes.

I know of a man killed driving his pickup a hundred miles an hour, and another who left his wife and family and ran off with a red-headed high school girl. They had been drinking applejack.

Now, when the birch and maple leaves have fallen and blow nervously around the roads, the juice from this year's apples has begun to ferment. This is no ordinary applejack. The bottles may remain hidden for years, deep down among the roots and the dead, before someone takes the first sip.

WAR SURPLUS

Aisle after aisle of canvas and khaki, helmets and mess kits, duffle bags, pea coats, gas masks... somewhere there is a whole field of abandoned aircraft, all kinds, P-38's, B-25's.... All you have to do is wait until dark, climb over the fence, pull the blocks from the wheels, climb in, start the engines and taxi out to the strip. It's easy. You can fly without ever having had a lesson.

A beautiful woman dressed in black sits on a bench near a grave. A tall man in dress uniform stands beside her and puts his hand on her shoulder. She says, "I come here often, it is so peaceful." He says, "Before John died, he asked me to look after you." They embrace. Behind them are many neat rows of white crosses extending over a green hill where the flag is flying proudly.

The engines make a deep drone; a comforting sound, and the light from the instrument panel tells you everything is stable and right. Below are silver-tufted clouds and tiny enemy towns, lovely toy towns, all lighted by the bomber's moon.

THE ICE FISHERMAN

From here he appears as a black spot, one of the shadows that today has found it necessary to assume solid form, and along with the black jut of shoreline far to the left, is the only break in the undifferentiated gray of ice and overcast sky. Here is a man going jiggidy-jig-jig in a black hole. Depth and the current are of only incidental interest to him. He's after something big, something down there that is pure need, something that, had it the wherewithal, would swallow him whole. Right now nothing is happening. The fisherman stands and straightens, back to the wind. He stays out on the ice all day.

INVISIBLE

There are moments when a person cannot be seen by the human eye. I'm sure you've noticed this. You might be walking down the street or sitting in a chair when someone you know very well, your mother or your best friend, walks past without seeing you. Later they'll say, "Oh, I must have been preoccupied." Not so. At times we are caught in a warp of space or time and, for a moment, vanish. This phenomenon occurs often among children and old people. No one understands exactly how this happens but some people remain invisible for long periods of time. Most of these do so by choice. They have learned to ride the moment, as a surfer rides the long curl of a wave. How exhilarating it is to ride like that, a feeling of triumph to move from room to room unseen, only the slightest breeze from your passing.

1988–1995

FISH OUT OF WATER

When he finally landed the fish it seemed so strange, so unlike other fishes he'd caught, so much bigger, more silvery, more important, that he half expected it to talk, to grant his wishes if he returned it to the water. But the fish said nothing, made no pleas, gave no promises. His fishing partner said, "Nice fish, you ought to have it mounted." Other people who saw it said the same thing, "Nice fish…." So he took it to the taxidermy shop but when it came back it didn't look quite the same. Still, it was an impressive trophy. Mounted on a big board the way it was, it was too big to fit in the car. In those days he could fit everything he owned into the back of his Volkswagen but the fish changed all that. After he married, a year or so later, nothing would fit in the car. He got a bigger car. Then a new job, children…. The fish moved with them from house to house, state to state. All that moving around took its toll on the fish, it began to look worn, a fin was broken off. It went into the attic of the new house. Just before the divorce became final, when he was moving to an apartment, his wife said, "Take your goddamn fish." He hung the fish on the wall before he'd unpacked anything else. The fish seemed huge, too big for this little apartment. Boy, it was big. He couldn't imagine he'd ever caught a fish that big.

NOVEMBER

I do not love the woods it occurs to me, the leafless, brushy, November popple and birch trees that stand around, stand around, crowding the peripheral vision. As if each were waiting to take its place in my consciousness and each falling back to become a part of the line that divides gray earth from gray sky, as undistinguished as gray hair.

Over there one shaft of sunlight penetrates the clouds as if it were an indicator: the finger of God pointing out...something. What is it Lord? More frozen trees? What is it? It's as if someone leaving on a train says something as the cars begin to move, something through the glass. I can see his lips moving. Gestures. What? I can't hear you. What?

A PORTRAIT OF THE MASTER

In this picture Jesus stands, as if addressing his followers, with his right arm partially raised, his index finger, slightly crooked, pointing upward. His left arm extends downward, palm open. He looks as he often does in pictures, white robe, sandals, beard neatly trimmed. His hair is rather long but clean. His face is calm, unwearied, because Jesus maintains, even thrives under the pressure of constant travel and the demands of those who flock to him. These are a ragged bunch, malcontents, the disenfranchised, those for whom heaven is impossible, the only ones who show any interest at all in what he has to say. They want help; they come to tell their stories, to ask questions, but mainly to listen. They have the sense that he is one of them, only better. And though the word he brings is difficult, it is the saying that is important. We must continually explain ourselves to ourselves. There is no one else to listen. He says again: "Here is the earth. Here is the sky."

FREEWAY

Just south of Hinkley a car passes me from behind.
I glance over at the driver. It's my old girlfriend from
25 years ago! Exactly the same, she hasn't aged
a day. The same blond, windblown and frazzled
hair, the same intent look. She's on her way back
to Oklahoma probably, all her stuff loaded inside.
She's on her way to get some money out of her ex,
or to some other desperate appointment that will
finally make the difference. Whatever I'm into now,
whatever I've become, she doesn't want to know.
She won't look at me. She knows that you can't
take your eyes off the road for even an instant.

INSECTS

Insects never worry about where they are or where they are going. A mosquito is so dedicated to the pursuit of warm blood that it neglects the long-range plan. If a mosquito follows you into the house it waits patiently until the lights are out and you are nearly asleep then it heads straight for your ear. Suppose you miss, hit yourself in the head and knock yourself out and the mosquito succeeds in drawing blood. How will it get out of the house again to breed? What are its chances?

Insects don't seem to have a sense of place but require only a certain ambiance. A fly that gets driven 500 miles in a car and then is finally chased out the window does not miss the town where it spent its maggothood. Wherever this is, it will be fine; a pile of dog shit, a tuna salad sandwich, a corpse.

IN THE STREETS

He carries everything he owns in a paper bag. What are you? A broken alarm clock? A returnable pop bottle? Once, on this very corner, a man hit him in the mouth. That's why some of his teeth are missing. It was drink made that man hit him. He never drinks. He waits for you every day with his hand out. Every day without fail. It's a wonder he's still alive. The coldest days he spends at the public library. But where does he go at night? The moon is shining now at four in the afternoon and down here it's all wind and shadows. In the streets with the blowing snow and newspapers he carries on the same argument with his parents, though they have been dead thirty years. At the mouths of alleys he pauses.… He is an only child. All he wants is his share.

THE CURE FOR WARTS

Draw a circle in red around the wart while repeating the incantation, words not to be spoken aloud in the presence of another human being. Once those words are spoken they are forever changed and you must begin again. A few special words to say to yourself in the silence and the dark. A phrase to worry over, polish and perfect, to believe in, despite all evidence to the contrary. In a few weeks the wart should drop off. But magic is so approximate. Perhaps only a wheel cover comes loose from your car as you drive down the interstate and rolls into the ditch. No chance of retrieving it in the heavy traffic. Later perhaps one of the ubiquitous crows will spot it there in the high grass and fly down to admire his reflection in the shiny surface. Beautiful. Fascinating. He opens his beak to sing. Yes, perhaps he'll sing.

AFTER SCHOOL

She had made a kind of promise to herself not to stop, but his house was right on her way home, besides, she thought, it was OK because they were just friends, they had always been just friends.... But, of course, he wasn't home when she knocked and his mother seemed like she was in a bad mood or something, but then his mother often seemed to be in a bad mood. Now it was nearly dark. Lights were on in some of the houses. The last sunlight shone red and orange on the bare birch trees and on the snowdrifts. It was beautiful, perfectly still, almost like a painting, she thought. And she was the one in the picture, walking home after school, always, toward supper and the long winter night.

THE LOST BOY

When Jason did not come home from school on the bus Barbara began to worry. She went next door to ask if Bobby, who rode the same bus, had seen Jason. Bobby remembered seeing Jason but didn't think he got on the bus. Bobby's mother, Teresa, said, "Oh, he probably just decided to walk." Teresa thought Barbara was a silly woman who fussed over her children. Bobby and Chris set out to look for Jason. It was an adventure, a search through the Dark Continent. Barbara used Teresa's phone to call the school. Meanwhile, Jason returned home, went in the back door and up to his room. Through the open window he could hear his mother in the next yard. He flopped down on the bed and looked at comics. He could hear his mother talking about calling the police. He lay looking at the big crack in the ceiling. He thought about what it was like to be lost. He thought he could hear voices, far away, calling his name.

GREEN TOMATO

This morning after the first frost, there is a green tomato among the Kleenex, combs and loose change, the more usual clutter on the dresser. That's the way it is around here—things picked up, put down, lost or forgotten. Here is the possibility of next year's crop, even more, in one green tomato. It makes me smile to see it there, newly discovered, confident and mysterious as the face of my young son who comes to the bedroom early, ready to play. There is no point in my telling you too much of what makes me happy or sad. I did not wake to find, at this moment, in this unlikely place, only my own life.

THE LANGUAGE OF CROWS

A crow has discovered a scrap of roadkill on the blacktop and can't resist telling everyone in a loud voice. Immediately another crow arrives on the scene and the fight begins, cawing, flapping, and biting. Suddenly crows come flying in from every direction to enter the battle, skimming low over the treetops, all cawing loudly. Finally one of the crows makes off with the prize and flies a few hundred yards into the trees. But as soon as he stops the others are on him and the fight begins again. This scene is repeated time after time and each time the crows move farther away into the woods until their cawing has grown faint but remains undiminished in intensity. Then suddenly here they are again, full-force and in your face. Crows have a limited vocabulary, like someone who swears constantly, and communication seems to be a matter of emphasis and volume.

If you lie quietly in bed in the very early morning, in the half-light before time begins and listen carefully, the language of crows is easy to understand. "Here I am." That's really all there is to say and we say it again and again.

WEST WIND

Trees fling themselves about in order to evict the noisy birds. A little boy leans into the wind and runs. He wants to fly with the crows. He flaps his arms and squawks. Mother is determined, runs after, grabs him and straps him into the stroller seat. "You stay right here." The little boy wants to fly like the wrapper from a hamburger, all brightly colored, into the busy sky.

So many plans, but the stakes are broken, the string knotted and tangled. Yet I feel a sense of accomplishment. I hold my car keys in my hand and it seems to me that I have just returned from a long trip.

WIND CHIME

Eventually someone will get sick of this clatter and will tie up the strings or remove the whole contraption. This instrument was meant for subtler sounds, silence and overtones, only the hint of a breeze, days in which the phone does not ring even once, long afternoons that fade into twilight with a single star there in the bell-clear western sky. I sigh and lay the book aside.... But the wind is unrelenting. It must have been like this long ago, a single sound over and over until at last someone sitting alone in the early dark became aware of it and realized what it means to be alive.

CORKSCREW

The woman next door comes over to return a corkscrew. "Thanks for letting us use this. I'm sorry you couldn't make it to the party." I don't remember being invited to a party. I stand looking at the thing dumbly as she goes. I don't recognize it. This isn't my corkscrew. Well, I don't really own this or anything else, really. That has become more apparent to me as time goes by. This is just another thing that came to my door of its own volition, out of some instinctual urge perhaps, the way bees swarm into a tree, piling up, forming what seems to be a single living shape; or came by accident, the way the wind makes a dust devil out of dirt and straw, whatever is at hand. It careens across the field, picks up a newspaper, picks up a driver's license, picks up a college degree…. "Margaret, I'd like you to meet Louis. He's not the guy I was telling you about." "Really? Who are you then?"

SAINTHOOD

Because of my extraordinary political correctness and sensitivity of late, I have been elevated to the status of Temporary Minor Saint (secular). The position comes with a commendation praising my "uncharacteristic reticence tantamount to sagacity." This means that my entire being is now suffused with a pale radiance somewhat like the light from a small fluorescent bulb, the light on a kitchen range perhaps, only not quite so bright, and that instead of walking I now float at an altitude of approximately three inches above the ground. I move at a slow and stately speed that befits my new rank. I move to the left or right by inclining my head and upper body in the appropriate direction. It's a less-than-perfect condition. The light keeps my wife awake at night and though the added elevation is somewhat beneficial, moving about in a crowd presents difficulties. My forward speed seems to be fixed and, though slow, is quite tricky to stop. I lean back but momentum carries me forward like a boat. Suddenly turning my head can send me veering into the person next to me or into a wall. In order to remain in one place I've found it necessary to attach cords to my belt on one end and to various solid objects around the room on the other. These days I take my meals standing up, tethered like the Hindenburg.

A POOL GAME

They share a cuestick. He breaks, makes the four ball and misses a shot on the six. He puts the cue down carefully, an archbishop surrendering the symbols of the church. He offers a few words of advice on her first shot. She picks up the cue as if it were the Olympic torch and starts off around the table. She puts away the nine, fifteen and the eleven. Bam. Bam. Bam. And this is for you. Pow! The ten. He sits at the bar, bored. He's been playing for so many years. She thinks the game has possibilities, just needs a little work, a little fixing up. She misses a shot on the twelve. He gets up slowly. She is trying to lug a large cement statue of St. Francis into the backyard by herself. He goes to help. Secretly though, it makes him mad. He'll have to fight through the Pacific from island to island again. He's such an old soldier. He picks up his weapon and goes after the deuce and the tray.

HOW TO TELL A WOLF FROM A DOG

A wolf trots along with his head down, tail down. He has a look of preoccupation, or worry, you might think. He has a family to support. He probably has a couple of broken ribs from trying to bring down a moose. He's not getting workman's comp, and no praise for his efforts, except perhaps slobbery kisses from the pups when he brings home some meat. The wolf looks unemployed, flat broke.

On the other hand, a dog of similar features, a husky or a malamute, has his head up, ears up, looks attentive, self-confident, cheerful and obedient. He is fully employed with an eye toward promotion. He carries his tail high, like a banner. He's part of a big organization and has the title of "man's best friend."

MR. WATKINS

When Mr. Watkins discovered one of the old gods dead in the crawl space under the house he put on his overalls, tied a bandanna over his nose and mouth and worked his way beneath the low cobweb-covered floor joists on his belly. He planned to drag it out by the heels but as soon as he touched the corpse there was a flash and a pop like a downed powerline. Mr. Watkins' heart stopped and the air smelled of ozone. The resulting fire completely destroyed the house and the garage.

Stray dogs, squirrels, flights of harpies roosting on the TV antenna, angels and devils only too ready to spirit you away....

At night Mr. Watkins used to patrol his 75 by 150 foot lot with a flashlight. You could hear his cough; see the light bobbing over the damp grass in summer, over the snowbanks in winter. Mr. Watkins was an old man and forgot things easily but he knew where the property lines were drawn and, by god, if you don't know that you don't know anything.

ADAM

At first it was okay naming the beasts of the field and the fowls of the air... dog, cat, cow... but it was a time-consuming job and after awhile it became boring... slender loris, bridled guillemot.... And the insects drove him crazy. Then there were the plants and rocks. Sunrise to sunset, the same thing. He didn't want to just name the things Jehovah had made. He wanted to recombine the elements to make something significant, a creation of his own. He just needed some time off to think, to plan. He wanted a convertible, something sporty, so he could take Eve for a little drive; lovely Eve dressed in her snakeskin miniskirt with the matching bag.

YOUR BABY

Cry and curse, stamp your foot down hard, because the surface of the earth is no more than a crust, a bunch of loose tectonic plates, something like the bones of a baby's skull, floating on a core of molten magma: chaos and anarchy, the fires of hell. And as you've been told repeatedly, it's all in your hands. It's like the egg you were given in Marriage and Family class. "This is your baby, take care of it." So dutifully you drew a smile face on, then as an afterthought added a pair of eyebrows shaped like rooftops. It gave the egg-baby a slightly sinister appearance. Then a friend added Dracula fangs and said, "See it looks just like its daddy." "Let me see" someone said and gave your elbow a shove....

Late at night. Where is your demon child now, as you sit dozing over the periodic tables?

ON AGING

There are no compensations for growing old, certainly not wisdom. And one gave up anticipating heaven long ago. Perhaps there is a kind of anesthesia resulting from short-term memory loss, from diminished libido, from apathy and fatigue that is mistaken for patience.

The rich can afford to grow old gracefully but the flesh of the poor shows each defeat like a photographic plate that records the movement of the planets and the stars and the rotation of the earth. Eyesight fails and hearing, the skin wrinkles and cracks, the bones twist, the muscles degenerate.... It takes all morning to open a can of soup.

The world collapses inward. Memory is no recompense. The past is fiction, a story of interest only to the young. There is only, as there always was, the moment. The instant, which, when you become aware of it, is blinding as the flash when someone snaps a picture of you blowing out the candles.

AUTOMOBILE REPAIR

It's raining and the car stalls with Mama, the kids and a full load of laundry inside. At least the warning lights still work. You raise the hood and find yourself staring, once again, into the void. Fuel pump? Alternator? The trick is to keep this thing running without spending any money, akin to making something from nothing. Thus Jehovah, confronted with a similar difficulty, simply began assembling the salvaged parts of the previous universe. Once you have located the problem you're ready (two or three cups of coffee will help) to plunge into the mud and grease. This time it's easy. The wire from the coil to the distributor has fallen off. It's running again— bald tires, broken exhaust, rust....

CAMPSITE

He paddles the canoe across the still water, alone in the evening, back to his camp. The water is perfect for walking, flat as the floor of a ballroom. This evening only the shadows of spruce and pine walk out from the forest, a time of darkening reflection. He pulls the canoe onto the shore and turns it over in just the way that his ancestors did. He builds a fire the way they did except that he uses matches and a few pieces of newspaper. He does not speak. His ancestors did not speak. They could only grunt and point. He does not know who his ancestors were except that they, like him, were notorious liars. He sits in a circle of light. An owl calls out from the trees. He sits in the smoke and pokes at the glowing coals with a stick. He moves a little to the left. The smoke follows him. He moves a little to the right.

THE GATE

The gate makes a few hesitant moves in the wind, some false starts that allow a few dry leaves to blow into the yard. Then as if suddenly determined to leave forever, the gate swings wide open, bounces off a snow bank and slams shut. It remains still for a time, as if stunned by the experience. Then it begins again, moving a few tentative inches before the big rush. The gate is teased by the wind. It's useless. The gate is set in its ways. It can only break at the hinges, splinter and fall down.

UNFORTUNATE LOCATION

In the front yard there are three big white pines, older than anything in the neighborhood except the stones. Magnificent trees that toss their heads in the wind like the spirited black horses of a troika. It's hard to know what to do, tall dark trees on the south side of the house, an unfortunate location, blocking the winter sun. Dark and damp. Moss grows on the roof, the porch timbers rot and surely the roots have reached the old bluestone foundation. At night, in the wind, a tree could stumble and fall, killing us in our beds. The needles fall year after year making an acid soil where no grass grows. We rake the fallen debris, nothing to be done. We stand around with sticks in our hands. Wonderful trees.

DRIFTWOOD

It is pleasant to lie on the rocky shore in the sun, exposed and open. It's all there—the sound of wind, the sound of waves—the meaningless journal of a lifetime. Nothing is clear, not even the obvious. One loses interest and falls asleep within the water's easy reach.

This driftwood on the beach, dry and bleached white, white as a bone you might say, or white as snow. If an artist (wearing a sweatshirt, blue jeans and tennis shoes without socks) came walking along, he might, seeing the possibilities, pick up this piece of driftwood and take it home. Not me. I fling it back in the water.

AMATEUR ARTIST

He sees that the eyes are wrong. The left eyelid should curve more. He erases and draws the line again. He has no ease with this, no grace, no freedom. It's like work. He wants to get it right. He looks at her photo again and then at the drawing. The drawing looks wrong, too stiff, and unnatural. He leaves the eyes and goes to the breasts. He likes this better, the easy graceful sweep of the pencil. Now he sees that the mouth is not right. The paper is nearly worn through in places from erasing and redrawing. How easily everything can go wrong. A misplaced mark becomes a deformity. Another mark, and the mood is completely changed. She looks out at him with eyes slightly askew and it's apparent that she is not pleased. Whoever this is.

VIBRATION

The windowpane vibrates at a constant, barely audible frequency. One doesn't notice it at first, but it can be quite annoying once you become aware of it. The water in this glass vibrates when I set it on the table—waves in a miniature ocean. The glass vibrates; therefore the table is moving. Put your fingers here or there and you can feel it. And the floor. Perhaps there is some large machine nearby working day and night, some tremendous project that never gets completed. If you look long enough at anything—the house next door, the leafless ash tree, the old woman in the ratty fur walking her overweight dog—you can see the slight blurring, a kind of blue-white outline, an uncertainty, a sadness as each thing separates itself from the air.

WINTER LIGHT

The sun glitters at a low angle through the bare trees, a distant January sun, light without warmth, making a pattern of stripes, varied widths of sunlight and shadow, across the road. The car moves like a scanner over a bar code. This is the tally of a very protracted shopping trip. Light and dark, light and dark.... It's the old duality: good and evil, male and female, dogs and cats, etc. The strobe light flashes of sun are hypnotic, dangerous, creating the illusion that the car is stopped and that the road is no more than a series of still photographs projected on a screen... or the opposite illusion—that you've been somewhere, that you are on your way somewhere.

NO HIRED MAN

It turns out that everything I've written is untrue. It wasn't entirely innocent. For instance, when I described a woman kneeling down near the creek, I knew that it wasn't a woman but a pile of brush, a few rags and some shreds of polyvinyl. Worse. When I think about it now I realize that there was no brush pile. No creek, either.

One evening after supper, when I was three or four years old, the hired man said "I'll make you something." He took a couple of brazing rods from the welder and spent a long time twisting them together with pliers. I tried to wait patiently. Then suddenly he said, "It won't work" and threw the thing on the pile of scrap metal outside the garage. After he had gone, walking the long road to town, I looked at the thing he'd made. I carried it around for awhile then put it back on the scrap heap. I never found out what he intended to make. Or what it was.

NO MATTER HOW FAR YOU DRIVE

I sat between Mamma and Daddy.
My sister sat on Mamma's lap.
Daddy drove. Fields, telephone poles....
I watched the sun go down.
"Never look straight at the sun,
it could ruin your eyes."
No matter how far you drive
you can't get to the sun.
I touched the pearly knob
of the gearshift lever
and felt the vibration in my fingers.
It made Daddy nervous.
'Never mess around with that.
You could ruin the car,
cause an accident."
It was dark, the sun gone to China.
Out there in the dark,
fourteen lights. I counted. Fourteen.
Rabbits ran in front of the car
from one black ditch to the other.
I didn't know where we were.
I could see the red light on the dashboard
and the light of Daddy's Lucky Strike
that broke into a million sparks behind us
when he threw it out the window.

EVENING

At evening the light
chooses carefully
the things it loves;
the water, the white
belly of the fish,
the hands of the fisherman,
the bright blade of the knife.

1996–2000

THE PROSE POEM

The prose poem is not a real poem, of course. One of the major differences is that the prose poet is incapable, either too lazy or too stupid, of breaking the poem into lines. But all writing, even the prose poem, involves a certain amount of skill, just the way throwing a wad of paper, say, into a wastebasket at a distance of twenty feet, requires a certain skill, a skill that, though it may improve hand-eye coordination, does not lead necessarily to an ability to play basketball. Still, it takes practice and thus gives one a way to pass the time, chucking one paper after another at the basket, while the teacher drones on about the poetry of Tennyson.

TOO MUCH SNOW

Unlike the Eskimos we only have one word for snow but we have a lot of modifiers for that word. There is too much snow, which, unlike rain, does not immediately run off. It falls and stays for months. Someone wished for this snow. Someone got a deal, five cents on the dollar, and spent the entire family fortune. It's the simple solution. It covers everything. We are never satisfied with the arrangement of the snow so we spend hours moving the snow from one place to another. Too much snow. I box it up and send it to family and friends. I send a big box to my cousin in California and one to Uncle Ralph in Texas. I send a small box to my mother. She writes, "Don't send so much. I'm all alone now, I'll never be able to use so much." To you I send a single snowflake, beautiful, complex and delicate: different from all the others.

A PLACE FOR EVERYTHING

It's so easy to lose track of things. A screwdriver, for instance. "Where did I put that? I had it in my hand just a minute ago." You wander vaguely from room to room, having forgotten, by now, what you were looking for; staring into the refrigerator, the bathroom mirror…"I really could use a shave…"

Some objects seem to disappear immediately while others never want to leave. Here is a small black plastic gizmo with a serious demeanor that turns up regularly, like a politician at public functions. It seems to be an "integral part" a kind of switch with screw holes so that it can be attached to something larger. Nobody knows what. It probably went with something that was thrown away years ago. This thing's use has been forgotten but it looks so important that we are afraid to throw it in the trash. It survives by bluff, like certain insects that escape being eaten because of their formidable appearance.

My father owned a large, three-bladed, brass propeller that he saved for years. Its worth was obvious, it was just that it lacked an immediate application since we didn't own a boat and lived hundreds of miles from any large bodies of water. The propeller survived all purges and cleanings, living, like royalty, a life of lonely privilege, mounted high on the garage wall.

NORTHERN LIGHT

Matisse and Monet had plenty of light. They were profligate, slopping Mediterranean sun everywhere. Vermeer had to buy it, a little at a time, import it from Africa or someplace. It ruined him, finally, the costly gold leaf and the precious ultramarine. In the north the light has to be concentrated and focused. Each detail must be accounted for, placed carefully just this side of darkness. Here a bit of sun on a yellow building and here light from the window, illuminating her face and highlighting the folds of her dress, the map on the wall, the letter in her hand. News from far away, we imagine. We can't know if it's good news or bad, but then, any word the light brings is better than no word at all.

THUNDERSTORM WARNING

The National Weather Service has issued a severe thunderstorm warning effective until two AM. Viewers should expect heavy rain, hail, damaging winds, dizziness, nausea, headache, fainting, disorientation, uncertainty, loss of direction and the questioning of deeply held beliefs. Persons in the warning area should seek shelter immediately. If you are caught out in the open you should lie face down in a ditch or a depression.

SOMERSAULT

Some children did handsprings or cartwheels. Those of us who were less athletically gifted did what we called somersaults, really a kind of forward roll. Head down in the summer grass, a push with the feet, then the world flipped upside-down and around. Your feet, which had been behind you, now stretched out in front. It was fun and we did it, laughing, again and again. Yet, as fun as it was, most of us, at some point, quit doing somersaults. We had more serious matters to attend to and so over the years we lost the knack. But only recently, someone at Evening Rest (Managed Care for Seniors) discovered the potential value of somersaults as physical and emotional therapy for the aged, a recapturing of youth, perhaps. Every afternoon, during the summer and early fall, weather permitting, the old people, despite their feeble protests, are led or wheeled onto the lawn, where each is personally and individually aided in the heels-over-head tumble into darkness. When the wind is right you can hear, even at this distance, the crying of those who have fallen and are unable to rise.

INDECISION

People died or moved away and did not return. His wife left and the dog ran away. Things broke and were not replaced. At one time he had owned a car and a telephone. No more. And yet somehow, things did not become more simple. Then one night, roused from sleep he stepped out naked into the below-zero winter night, into the clear midnight and 20 billion stars. Nothing stirred, not a leaf, nothing out there, not the animal self, not the bird-brained self. Not a breath of wind, yet somehow the door slammed shut locking behind him and knocking the kerosene lantern to the floor. Suddenly the whole place was afire. What to do? Should he try to make the mile-long run through the woods over hard-crusted snow to the nearest neighbor, or just stick close to his own fire and hope that someone would see the light? The cabin was going fast. Flames leaped high above the bare trees.

FEBRUARY

for Michael Van Walleghen

Snow falls upon snow. It piles up on the roads, mile after gray mile of it catches in the wheel wells of the car. It piles up like debt, like failure, and, as your mother pointed out, you've put on a few pounds since Christmas. Now in February the winter seems permanent, glacial. Each snowfall is more a feeling than an external event, a heaviness, shortness of breath. You wake in a panic, tearing at the blankets. It's only a cat. A large house cat. You've wakened in an overheated room in a strange house with the family cat sleeping on your chest. You are a guest, you don't belong here. Heart pounding, you want to be on your way. But it's the middle of the night, in winter. There's no place to go. You won't be here very long. Relax. Nothing has changed. You are who you've always been, only more so.

STONE ARCH, NATURAL ROCK FORMATION

It is higher, more narrow, more treacherous than we imagined. And here we are in a spot where there's no going back, a point of no return. It has become too dangerous to continue as we have. We simply are not as sure-footed and nimble as we were when we started out. There's nothing to do but sit down, carefully, straddling the rock. Once seated, I'm going to turn slightly and hand the bag of groceries back to you. Then I'm going to scoot ahead a few inches and turn again. If you then lean forward carefully and hand me the bag you will be able to move ahead to the spot I previously occupied. It is a miserably slow process and we still have the problem of the steep descent on the other side. But if we are patient, my love, I believe we will arrive safely on the ground again a few yards from where we began.

THE TELEPHONE

In the old days telephones were made of rhinoceros tusk and were big and heavy enough to be used to fight off an intruder. The telephone had a special place in the front hallway, a shrine built into the wall, a nicho previously occupied by the blessed virgin, and when the phone rang it was serious business. "Hello." "One if by land and two if by sea." "What? "Unto you a child is born." "What?" "What did he say?" "Something about the Chalmers' barn." The voice was carried by a single strand of bare wire running from coast to coast, wrapped around a Coke bottle stuck on a tree branch, dipping low over the swamp, it was the party line, all your neighbors in a row, out one ear and in another. "We have a bad connection, I'm having trouble understanding you."

Nowadays telephones are made of recycled plastic bags and have multiplied to the point where they have become a major nuisance. The phone might ring at you from anywhere, the car, the bathroom, under the couch cushions.... Everyone hates the telephone. No one uses the telephone anymore so telephones, out of habit or boredom or loneliness perhaps, call one another. "Please leave a message at the tone." "I'm sorry, this is a courtesy call. We'll call back at a more convenient time. There is no message."

A PATCH OF OLD SNOW

Here's a patch of snow nestled in the roots of a spruce tree, a spot the sun never touches. Mid-May and there's still snow in the woods. It's startling to come upon this old snow on such a warm day. It is the record of another time. It's something like coming across a forgotten photograph of yourself. The stylish clothes of the period look silly now. And your haircut! Awful. You were young, wasteful, selfish, completely mistaken and, probably, no less aware than today.

FIRE DANGER

When conditions are right, it takes only the smallest spark to set the entire forest on fire. Like love, kindled by the merest glance or a smile, even though the two of you have nothing at all in common. It's the chance arrangement of positive and negative ions. You say, "We have so much in common, so much more than Elaine and I ever have." You say, "Sometimes we talk for hours. We have so much to talk about." All summer, all through September and October the winds stirred in the dry timber. Now in November, the leaves are down, and the cold rain falls day after day. "So what?" you say to yourself, "So what?" You tell your friends, "It's wonderful. I've never felt like this before. I'm so unhappy." And your friends run away when they see you coming.

THE FISHING LURE

I've spent a great deal of my life fretting over things that most people wouldn't waste their time on. Trying to explain things I haven't a clue about. It's given me that worried look, that wide-eyed, staring look. The look that wild animals sometimes have, deer for instance, standing in the middle of the highway trying to make sense of the situation: "What is that?" Motionless, transfixed. The same look that's on the face of the fishing lure. Stupidity? Terror? What is the right bait for these conditions? High cirrus clouds, cold front moving in. It's all a trick anyway. What is this thing supposed to be? A minnow? A bug? Gaudy paint and hooks all over. It's like bleached blond hair and bright red lipstick. Nobody really believes it. There isn't a way in the world I'd bite on that thing. But I might swim in just a little closer.

STORY

The things that happen willy-nilly in life, lawsuit, gum disease, romance…must be given, if not meaning, at least some context. Each has to be incorporated immediately into the story you tell yourself, and the sooner the better. In order to avoid unpleasant surprises, things should be written in before they occur. But now I've gotten ahead of myself. There I am, my future self, my shadow stretching out thirty feet ahead on the winter road: enormous feet, wide legs, big fat ass and a torso tapering away to a tiny pin head. This is not a true likeness, of course, the distortion caused by my distance from the sun. But it gives you the idea. The truth, the absolute truth, is like absolute zero, more a hypothesis than an actuality. If you could experience it you wouldn't like it. It's cold enough as it is. The truth is an imaginary point, like the vanishing point. It's as if there were a point to this story. As if when you got to the end you could remember what happened in the beginning.

CHANGE

All those things that have gone from your life, moon boots, TV trays and the Soviet Union, that seem to have vanished, are really only changed. Dinosaurs did not disappear from the earth but evolved into birds and crock pots became bread makers and then the bread makers all went to rummage sales along with the exercise bikes. Everything changes. It seems at times (only for a moment) that your wife, the woman you love, might actually be your first wife in another form. It's a thought not to be pursued…. Nothing is the same as it used to be. Except you, of course, you haven't changed…well, slowed down a bit, perhaps. It's more difficult nowadays to deal with the speed of change, disturbing to suddenly find yourself brushing your teeth with what appears to be a flashlight. But essentially you are the same as ever, constant in your instability.

CORONADO

Coronado came up from Mexico in search of a life of the imagination. The Zunis said "Oh God, here comes Coronado and those Spaniards." The Zunis drew a line on the ground with cornmeal and said, "OK Coronado cross that line and you'll be sorry." But of course he crossed. The Zunis said, "Seven Cities of Gold? Go see the Pueblos." So on he went, but the great cities did not appear, only mud houses. The Pueblos said "Oh yeah, the Seven Cities of Gold, they're over northeast, way over, maybe five hundred or a thousand miles." So he set out again. There was nothing, day after day, no gold, no silver, not even an ATM, just the wind blowing through the prairie grass. Coronado was a determined man who knew that hard work and patience would be rewarded. But when he got to Kansas he realized that this had to be a joke or else that someone had been badly misinformed.

SEPTEMBER

for Phil Dentinger

One evening the breeze blowing in the window
turns cold and you pull the blankets around you.
The leaves of the maples along Wallace Avenue
have already turned red and someone you loved
does not come around anymore. That's all right,
you tell yourself, things change with the cycle of
the seasons and evolve. A mistake, a wrong turn
takes you somewhere else, someplace new.

But perhaps there are forces other than chance
at work here. Perhaps a person changes
deliberately out of boredom with the present
condition. Perhaps our children, from a desire
to become simply other than what we are, grow
feathers, learn to breathe underwater or to see
in the dark.

JAZZ POEM

I always wanted to write one of those Jazz poems. You know the kind, where it's three a.m. in some incredibly smoky, out of the way, little club in Chicago or New York, April 14, 1954 (it's always good to give the date) and there are only a few sleepy people left in the place, vacant tables with half-empty glasses, overturned chairs... and then Bird or Leroy or someone plays this incredible solo and it's like, it's like...well, you just should have been there. The poet was there and you understand from the poem that jazz is hip, intellectual, cool, but also earthy and soulful, as the poet must be, as well, because he really digs this stuff. Unfortunately, I grew up listening to rock and roll and decidedly unhip country music and it just doesn't work to say you should have been in Gary Hofstadter's rec room, July 24, 1961, sipping a Pepsi, listening to Duane Eddy's latest album and playing air guitar.

A MIRACLE

When my father was eight he cut his foot on a broken bottle hidden in the tall grass and got blood poisoning. Inexorably the red line rose toward the heart and the doctors could do nothing. Then one evening just at dark the gypsy healer came to the door. No one had called her, an old woman with many layers of odd clothes, long skirts, scarves and a man's raincoat. She examined the foot, muttered some words, a prayer perhaps, and said "Here. The poison is here." She made a swift cut with a small knife that seemed to appear suddenly in her hand. "You must soak the foot in very hot water and Epsom salts for one hour, three times a day. In three days the child will be well." And it worked. The healer stopped by each day around sunset to examine the wound. Strangely, she would take no pay. She went back to the gypsy camp, to the horses and wagons, the dark-skinned men in white shirts, the ragged children. One morning, a week later, my grandfather woke to find that all the chickens were gone, every single one, only some feathers on the floor of the silent coop. The gypsies were gone too, vanished in the night. Miracles always have a cost. When one thing is repaired another breaks. When something is healed, something else dies. So the old woman took nothing, knowing God would provide.

THE COUPLE

They no longer sleep quite as well as they did
when they were younger. He lies awake thinking
of things that happened years ago, turning
uncomfortably from time to time, pulling on the
blankets. She worries about money. First one
and then the other is awake during the night,
in shifts as if keeping watch, though they can't
see very much in the dark and it's quiet. They
are sentries at some outpost, an abandoned fort
somewhere in the middle of the Great Plains
where only the wind is a regular visitor. Each
stands guard in the wilderness of an imagined
life in which the other sleeps untroubled.

MUDHOLE

Life has no meaning. Right at the center of anything you can name there's a big nothing, a hole large enough to drive a truck through. But nobody dies just because of that. My grandfather farmed for years around a mudhole right in the middle of his already meager acreage. A kind of curving ditch known as "the creek," though it seldom held any water. The mark of the harrow and the mark of the plow followed the contour of the bank making a pleasing pattern in the dirt. The way the lines of a poem are pleasing (something about seagulls, the sun going down and the dust behind the tractor, rising in a tall column so that it was visible even from the County Line Bar two miles away) or like bars of music which has no meaning either. Someone can take a perfectly good drinking song, turn it into an anthem. People enlist, and things get a whole lot worse. But meanwhile, back at the tavern, the music goes on and so does the drinking.

DULUTH

"A baby, eh?" That's all he says. She never says he's the father but they get married anyway. This way the city gains another citizen. But for each one that's born another dies or moves away and things remain pretty much the same. The mayor has been dead for several years but we think he does a better job that way and we keep him in office. Once in awhile Bob Dylan comes back to town, but he never calls. We prefer it quiet, understated. At one o'clock Sunday morning the snow plow passes with its flashing blue light and then, ten minutes later, a car, silent, muffled by the snow. A light still shines in the attic apartment of a large house two blocks over. These old houses, once the mansions of mining millionaires and lumber barons, are full of secrets. Some properties have been completely restored and in others people keep bears as pets. If you are outside around dawn you might catch a glimpse of someone taking the bear for a walk and think "Why would anyone want a big dog like that? But then," you tell yourself, "there are all these new people in town."

A HILL OF BEANS

As children we were given inaccurate information. Things turned out to be much different than we were led to believe. Adults were not entirely to blame for this because most of them had no more idea what was going on than we did and found themselves bewildered at every turn, baffled by the impossible complexities of life. So instead of real insight we were given aphorisms. Gems such as, "life is no bed of roses" or "you can lead a horse to water but you can't make him drink." Of course, society has changed radically, even in my lifetime. Therefore the rather agrarian quality of these sayings has caused them to lose some of their original impact. "You aren't going to amount to a hill of beans." Which, to me, suggests laziness, shiftlessness, failure, poverty, rambling discourse, idle speculation... I suspect that "a hill of beans" refers to the fact that beans are of little value even in large quantities and also that they make very poor hills. Yet, I can't help imagining a really important hill, a great Bunker Hill of beans, or a San Juan Hill of slippery pork and beans up which a frustrated Teddy Roosevelt is trying to charge.

ICE

Walking on the icy pavement demands your attention. You have to learn to read the color, the texture, learn where you can safely step, learn to watch for the smooth, almost invisible ice or ice hidden by a light dusting of snow. Suddenly you're flat on your back. Children don't worry about falling. Their bodies are flexible and resilient and they have a shorter distance to fall. They fall, jump up and continue running. It's nothing. If a person of my age and size falls it makes a considerable impact. It's painful and embarrassing. Once I fell in front of the hardware store downtown, just like that, both feet straight out in front of me. Passersby gave me a strange look, not concern, more like disbelief. What is this guy doing? The very old, old women on high-risk shopping trips, old men shoveling snow on rooftops, seem to have forgotten the ice entirely. If their frail bodies were caught by the least wind they would skitter and clatter over the hard surface for miles.

BONES

The leaves have fallen, the geese have flown south and your hair has turned gray. Most of the people who knew you when you were a baby are dead now. Whatever it was caused them to stand up and walk around as if they knew where they were going has flown also. Something caused them to hesitate, turn back to the house, then begin again, slamming the screen door behind. That impulse has gone. Nothing remains now but bones, the skeptical bones. Soon snow will come to cover them again. No one has coffee ready, there are no fields to plow and they know all about you, shuffling around in the dry leaves. "It's only that kid up there, no reason to get up."

THE NAME

Instead of an idea a name comes to you, a name that no longer has any connection to the owner of the name. It comes as sound merely, rhythmic, musical, exotic and foreign to your ears, a sound full of distance and mystery. A name such as Desmond Tutu, Patrice Lumumba or Kofi Annan. You forget the names of acquaintances and the name of your first true love but this name comes to you. It repeats like a tune in your head. It refuses to go away, becomes a kind of mental mumbling. You say it to yourself over and over. This is your mantra, "Boutros Boutros-Ghali...." Then suddenly as it came, the name vanishes.

Deep in the night, long after your own name has flown away, a voice wakes you from a sound sleep, a voice clear and certain as the voice that summoned Elijah, saying "Oksana Baiul."

JANUARY

Daytime highs are well below zero. The air is absolutely clear and dry, the wind sharp, precise. We walk about in our bulky clothes like spacemen or old-fashioned divers on the bottom of the sea. The snow crunches underfoot. Now, above a single bare birch tree in the middle of a field of untrodden snow, the evening star appears in a most extraordinary blue sky. Everything is hard-edged, clear-cut. A perfect world made of glass. The sky is the exact color of Mary Beth Anderson's eyes. Beautiful, perfect. Perfect hair and perfect teeth. It always seemed that she knew exactly what she wanted and where she was going, that she had planned her life in detail. One thing I know for sure, she would have had no time for anyone who dresses the way we do.

IRON

Iron is purely masculine, containing perhaps too many Y chromosomes. Iron lacks the flexibility and strength of steel, which is tempered by the feminine element. Iron lacks delicacy, but does not lack courage. Iron is hard work and sweat. Iron is heavy-handed. Iron is passion without finesse. A long time ago a man discovered that he could make an impressive sound by dragging a large piece of iron through a field of stones. Iron is divorce, child-support payments, poorly planned crime, dishes in the sink, wool socks drying over the coal stove. Out back there's the hulk of a '57 Chevy still awaiting restoration. What glowed red hot in youth is cold as a pump handle in middle age.

A BEAR AND HIS MONEY

Every fall before he goes to sleep a bear will put away five or six hundred dollars. Money he got from garbage cans, mostly. People throw away thousands of dollars every day, and around here a lot of it goes to bears. But what good is money to a bear? I mean, how many places are there that a bear can spend it? First you have to locate the bear's den, in fall after the leaves are down. Back on one of the old logging roads you'll find a tall pine or spruce covered with scratch marks, the bear runes, which translate to something like "Keep out. That means you!" You can rest assured that the bear and his money are nearby, in a cave or in a space dug out under some big tree roots. Though sometimes the young males just flop down on the ground. You have to be careful. When you return in winter, a long hike on snowshoes, the bear will be sound asleep… In a month or two he'll wake, groggy, out of sorts, ready to bite something, ready to rip something to shreds… but by then you'll be long gone, back in town, spending like a drunken sailor.

WIND IN THE TREES

You could live on the go like the wind with what seems like a purpose or at least a direction, but no home, reckless, pushy, with an attention deficit disorder, no more than a name, really. People will say, "That guy, you know…." But if you stand still long enough you will be given an identity. You could live like the trees, parochial, rooted and restless, prone to hysteria. You could write letters to the editor. Living in the woods you get a lot of ideas about what God is up to, and what is going on in Washington. You'd have a family. Parents, grandparents, aunts and uncles all close around you until, if you are lucky, they recede, one by one, into the peripheral haze of memory. Finally, some space, a clearing, a place to fall.

HIGH FINANCE

"It takes money to make money," my father said, "you have to have something to invest." We all nodded and made affirmative, muttering sounds. "Take care of the nickels and the dollars will take care of themselves," my mother said. "Some people are born with a talent for making money," my father said, "but you've got to have a start, a little bit of luck," "Thrift. Thrift and hard work," Mother said, "that's what my parents taught me." We all stared silently into our coffee cups. "Owning your own business," Father said, as if he hadn't heard Mother at all, "that's the way to make money. You'll never make any money working for someone else." "Nonsense," Mother said. "That's all pie in the sky." "Pie in the sky," we thought, "mmm… pie in the sky!" Pie with great cumulus mounds of ice cream, served on silver platters, inside those castles in the air. Pie in the sky… cloudberry pie.

PIONEER FARM

Think of spending the winter alone here, in this two-room cabin. Think of spending it here with someone else. The settlers were frugal. They used newspaper for toilet tissue, newspaper for chinking between the logs, the words carefully mouthed and puzzled over then shoved into a crack. Once a month someone made the long trip into town to sell the eggs and buy a newspaper. They used feedbags for dresses, harness leather for door hinges, snot for bubble gum. The Bible was their only book. Mother was crazy and Father was a tyrant. The eldest daughter ran off with a sewing machine salesman. The first son ran away and set up his own little monarchy, just like this one. Everyone is gone now, even the owl who used roost in the barn. It's not a good place for a farm, the growing season too short, the ground too rocky. What I hate most is the lingering sanctimonious air, the condescending forgiveness.

THE PREACHER

When times were hard, no work on the railroad, no work down on the farm, some of my ancestors took to preaching. It was not so much what was said as the way in which it was said. The horn shall sound and the dog will bark and though you be on the highest mountain or down in the deepest valley when the darkness comes then you will lie down, and as the day follows the night you will surely rise again. The Lord our God hath summoned the saints and the angels and hath created both heaven and earth. Oh, my dear brothers and sisters we know so well the ways of this world, think then what heaven must be like. It required some thuses and haths and thous. It required a certain presence, a certain authority. The preacher was treated with respect and kept at a bit of a distance, like a rattler. There wasn't much money in it but it was good for maybe a dozen eggs or a chicken dinner now and then.

RADIO

When I was a kid I listened to the radio late at night. I tuned it low as I could and put my ear right up next to it because my dad didn't like it. He'd say, "Turn off that radio. It's after midnight!" No matter how low I tuned it he could still hear, from down the hall and through two closed doors. He was tired; it had been a long day his muscles ached but still he was nervous, on edge and this was just one more thing, the final thing, keeping him from the sleep, the absolute dead silence he wanted. As for me, whatever music I was listening to, some rock station way down on the border, probably, (100,000 watts of pure power!) has become even more faint over the years. But I can still hear it.

TUMBLING TUMBLEWEEDS

Out on the Oklahoma Plains, where I was born, the wind blows constantly. When I was a kid I'd get 35 cents and run as hard as I could to the Lotta-Burger or the movie theatre only to find it had blown away. Going home was no better. Sometimes it would take a couple of days to find my house. Under these conditions it was impossible to get acquainted with the neighbors. It was a shock to open the front door and be faced with the county jail, the Pentecostal Church or Aunt Erma carrying two large suitcases. Trash from all over the state caught and piled up in the yard and sometimes during the windiest times of spring, whole days blew away in a cloud of dust. I feel my natural lifespan may have been shortened by the experience. Still, it was a great place to grow up. As the old boy said, "You can have those big cities, people all jammed together. Give me some wide-open spaces." In the morning out on the plains you have a couple of cups of coffee, get all wound up and go like hell across an open field, try to bounce, clear both ditches and the highway so you don't get caught in the barbed wire, fly from one fenced-in nothing to another, hit the ground and keep on rolling.

THE SPEAKER

The speaker points out that we don't really have much of a grasp of things, not only the big things, the important questions, but the small everyday things. "How many steps up to your front door? What kind of tree grows in your back yard? What is the name of your district representative? What did you have for breakfast? What is your wife's shoe size? Can you tell me the color of your sweetheart's eyes? Do you remember where you parked the car?" The evidence is overwhelming. Most of us never truly experience life. "We drift through life in a daydream, missing the true richness and joy that life has to offer." When the speaker has finished we gather around to sing a few inspirational songs. You and I stand at the back of the group and hum along since we have forgotten most of the words.

OLD MAN WINTER

Old man Winter doesn't like anything. He doesn't like dogs or cats, or squirrels, or birds (especially seagulls), or children, or smart-ass college students. He doesn't like loggers or environmentalists, or snowmobilers, or skiers in their stupid spandex outfits. He doesn't like Christmas, or television, or newspapers for that matter. He doesn't like lawyers or politicians. There is a thing or two he could say to the host of the local talk-radio show but he knows for a fact that the son-of-a-bitch does the broadcast from his condo in Florida. He's pissed off about the OPEC oil conspiracy and the conspiracy of gas station owners to raise prices. He can't stand the current administration and didn't much like the last one, either. He doesn't like foreigners. And he doesn't like his neighbors (not that he has many); and when they finally die they just leave their junk all over the yard. He doesn't like that. He doesn't like the look of the sky right now, either, overcast, a kind of jaundice color. He hates that. And that stand of spruce trees behind the house turning black in the dusk... The way it gets dark earlier every day. He doesn't like that.

PAINTING AND WRITING

I have a letter written by my great-great-grandfather in 1902, full of the moment: "There are several cases of smallpox reported in Frederick." Yet despite the distance, the changes, there is an immediacy in the language. "Sim (a son-in-law) has sold $600 worth of wheat. He's thinking of buying a new buggy. I'm helping him paint his barn." It takes forever to paint one of those big barns. I think if I could find the place—somewhere southwest of Lyons—they'd still be at work, Sim on the high wooden ladder painting traditional barn red and the old man on the ground, painting the white trim around the doors and windows. So much work going into a structure that will fall down in fifty years, or less. It's awkward, difficult for any of us to know what to say. The past and the future are the same, finally. A time where you aren't. And you do what you do because it's the thing that you do.

"Well, this has certainly been interesting. Now, whose boy are you again...? Well, anyhow I'd better get back to work. This barn won't wait."

"No. You can't let your brush dry out."

"Yes, use it or lose it, as they say. Ha, ha. Say hello to everyone...."

BEAUTIFUL CHILD

People exclaim "What a pretty little girl!" But whenever a stranger speaks to her, she buries her face in her mother's lap or puts on a frown, looks away and refuses to answer. When she is alone, she sings a little song. She pushes back her long blond hair. She pretends to be a ballerina or perhaps the lady on the tight-rope high above an audience that is invisible there in the dark. As she takes her first delicate step into the spotlight the crowd breaks into applause…. Years later her boyfriend asks, "What's wrong tonight?" They have walked far down the beach and it occurs to him that she is angry. "Did I do something?" It's a question he asks frequently. "It's nothing," she says. Then there is a long silent moment. "You wouldn't understand." She looks far away across the water.

PERSONAL HISTORY

One has a feeling of having not lived life to its fullest, having not really accomplished anything, and at the same time there is a feeling of regret for past sins, those things one would like to undo. And all the while the years passing, passing, turning to decades, centuries. Civilizations rise and fall. Think of the Hittites. At one time they were the hottest power in the world, a practical, down-to-earth people, but one that did little, finally, to advance human civilization. What would a Hittite say if you met on the street?
"Listen, I'd like to apologize for those unwanted advances I made."
"That's all right. It was a long time ago."
"Nevertheless, I feel uneasy about it. It was rude and selfish of me. It's just that you were so...."
"It's OK, really. I can honestly say I never think of it."

BERRY PICKING

This time of year, mid-summer, we drive out the Matson road to pick thoughtberries, so called because once you spend a day picking you will think twice about ever doing it again. Thoughtberries don't grow in the deep woods but on the marginal, burned-over ground, in the scrub and scrap, in those awful swampy, bug-infested thickets out where the blackflies eat you alive. Thoughtberries are not plentiful. Sometimes it takes an hour of hard labor, picking the low stickery bushes to gather just a handful. Their scarcity must be most of their appeal because, really, they aren't all that good. Small, tough and sour, they need a lot of sugar to make them palatable. There are not enough of them in these parts to make them a commercially viable product, but then in many parts of the country they don't grow at all.

FLORIDA

This morning at the university I passed a young woman in the hall who was wearing a very tight orange t-shirt with FLORIDA printed on the front in large white letters. Naturally I thought of citrus fruit. I thought of orange groves with workers tending the smudge pots on cold nights. I thought of Wallace Stevens in his white suit, walking barefoot on the beach, carrying his shoes with the socks tucked inside, and I imagined the moon over Miami. I have never been to Florida but I know there are drug dealers, red tide, walking catfish, Republicans, Disney World, alligators, Walmart.... Still, the citrus fruit is very good this time of year and when I peel an orange and look out the window at the snow and the rough spruce trees it seems like a miracle. One taste and I know there is a world beyond my imagining. It's impossible, like love, yet it really exists.

BELIEF

We all have certain things we believe in. Usually they don't amount to much. Some people believe that if you put a spoon in the open bottle, champagne will keep its fizz. Others believe that hot water will freeze faster than cold, or that when you flush a toilet in the southern hemisphere the water always turns clockwise. Some people believe that you should wear a beanie and others believe in funny collars. In the absence of anything better these beliefs serve to separate your life from others lurking in the forest around you, like scent marking. People have certain phrases they like to use: "at the end of the day," or "on the same page," and words such as paradigm, trope, facilitator, objecthood.... Words that don't mean anything. We drop them like breadcrumbs to mark the way home—where we all intend to return one day.

THE WAVES

The east wind has risen today and the waves rise up. Praise to all rising up! To the life that seemed might never return after so many days of dead calm. The wind sends wave after wave scudding toward the shore where the ragged tufts of grass cling to the rock. Waves. I recognize some of these waves. They lift from the void, white-haired but determined, as if each had a purpose, a private destiny, someplace to go. (Brunch? A board meeting?) Once the savior walked across the water to give each wave, personally, a hand up. Perhaps he is returning even now, but the road to the shore is long, long…. The waves break and fall face forward, losing touch, losing credibility, losing all pretense of dignity.

ROCK COLLECTING

On Hegberg Road I found a really big agate, big as my fist, half buried in the dirt. I dug it out using a sharp rock as a digging tool. It took nearly fifteen minutes to dislodge the stone from the roadbed. I washed off the dirt in the ditch water and on closer examination I discovered that it wasn't an agate after all, just an ordinary reddish-colored rock, jasper maybe. What a relief! I could drop the rock back in the road. I could go on with my life.

JACK B. NIMBLE

The only light is the light you carry. You can feel the darkness coming up close behind. If you turn suddenly the darkness jumps back, the way the lion retreats momentarily from the desperate wildebeest. Once you were a beacon. Once you set the candlestick atop your head and did the rumba, the cha cha, the limbo, until the wee hours of the morning. You hold that candle so carefully in front of you that it makes strange shadows and lines across your face, but honestly, I've never seen you looking better. And that new suit, I think, works wonders.

NOVEMBER AGAIN

November again and the snow comes sudden and heavy. This is what we like best. This is what we paid our money for. Snow on snow, all day and all night, everything muffled, distant. Tomorrow, no school, no work, no worship service, no visitation of the sick, the poor, the widows or the orphans. Whatever it was, nothing can be done about it now. Your old position has been filled. Your footsteps have been filled. The roads are filled, drifted shut. Finally, even the directions are obliterated in the heavy snowfall.

FLIGHT

Past mishaps might be attributed to an incomplete understanding of the laws of aerodynamics or perhaps to an even more basic failure of imagination, but were to be expected. Remember, this is solo flight unencumbered by bicycle parts, aluminum and nylon or even wax and feathers. A tour de force, really. There's a lot of running and flapping involved, and as you get older and heavier, a lot more huffing and puffing. But on a bright day like today, with a strong headwind blowing up from the sea, when, having slipped the surly bonds of common sense and knowing she is watching, waiting in breathless anticipation, you send yourself hurtling down the long, green slope to the cliffs, who knows? You might just make it.

2001–2005

DINER

The time has come to say goodbye, our plates empty except for our greasy napkins. Comrades, you on my left, balding, middle-aged guy with a ponytail, and you, Lefty, there on my right, with the pack of cigarettes rolled up in your t-shirt sleeve, though we barely spoke I feel our kinship. You were steadfast in passing the ketchup, the salt and pepper, no man could ask for better companions. Lunch is over—the cheeseburgers and fries, the Denver sandwich—the counter nearly empty. Now we must go our separate ways. Not a fond embrace, but perhaps a hearty handshake. No? Well then, farewell. It is unlikely I'll pass this way again. Unlikely we will all meet again on this earth, to sit together beneath the neon and fluorescent calmly sipping our coffee, like the sages sipping their tea beneath the willow, sitting quietly, saying nothing.

FREE LAWN MOWER

There's a broken down lawn mower at the curbside with a sign "FREE." And so I ask myself, what does freedom mean to a lawn mower? A lawn mower that has only one job and no outside interests, a job which it can no longer perform properly? Gone the days of the engine's roar, the cloud of blue smoke, the open lawn, the waves of cut grass left in its wake, the flying gravel, the mutilated paper cup. Freedom could only mean the freedom to rust away into powder and scale. Most likely the lawn mower will be thrown into the back of a beat-up truck by a guy who sees its potential as scrap or who thinks he can make it work again, a guy who will seize upon anything of the even the slightest value, anything free.

THE BODY AND THE SOUL

Long ago I was told that the body was the temple of the soul, a temporal dwelling for the eternal soul. I suppose the body could be thought of as a dwelling, it has plumbing and electricity, it groans and creaks in the night. I think in most cases, however, it's more like a modest bungalow than a temple. And the house idea does not accommodate human mobility. Perhaps a motor home would be a better analogy. The body is the motor home of the soul, where the soul sits behind the wheel and drives the body here and there, back and forth to work, off to the seashore or the Rocky Mountains. But the soul is a bad driver, so often distracted, dwelling on higher things, pondering, moving slowly up the pass, traffic backed up behind for miles. The soul gazes idly out the windows (eyes) paying no attention whatsoever to the road, and is in danger of sending the entire metaphor plunging over the precipice.

KNIFE ISLAND

From Stoney Point it appears as a green, rounded shape in Superior's waters, perhaps safe haven, the Promised Land, like the Lake Isle of Innesfree rising from the mist. Up close it's just a pile of rocks with a few stunted trees, a place beaten by water and wind; a squalor of seagulls. The whole place is covered with gulls, gull shit, feathers and broken eggs, gulls in the air, gulls on the water, gulls on the ground. It's a noisy place, threat and intimidation, outrage, and indignation, the constant squabbling over territory. They cry, "justice!" "You are in my space!" Seagulls, like humans, not comfortable alone, not happy together. This is life with all its horrible enthusiasm, better seen from a distance.

OF AN AGE

I'm getting to an age when if I suddenly dropped dead most people would not be overly surprised. And, no doubt, there are some who would welcome the news. I'm not particularly looking forward to it—death and whatever comes after. Which is not much by the look of it, decomposition and discorporation, when all the microorganisms that makeup this conglomerate go their separate ways, thus ending one instance of corporate greed and mismanagement. But possibly some will linger, talk of an employee buyout, some wearing buttons that say "Solidarity Forever." Most likely, there will be a few farewell parties with drinks and reminiscing, balloons, a joke sign saying, "Will the last to leave please turn out the lights?"

OLD FRIENDS

There's a game we play, not a game exactly, a sort of call and response. It's one of the pleasures of living for a long time in a fairly small place. "You know, they lived over by Plett's Grocery." "Where that bank is now?" "That's right." "Plett's. I'd almost forgotten. Do you remember where Ward's was?" "Didn't they tear it down to build the Holiday Mall?" "Yes." "I remember. The Holiday Mall." It works for people, too. "Remember the guy who came to all the art exhibit openings, the guy with the hat?" "Yeah, he came for the free food and drinks?" "Right." "And there was the guy with the pipe and the tweed jacket who always said hello to everyone because he wasn't sure who he actually knew." "Oh, yes!" It's like singing an old song, la, la, la, and you actually remember some of the words. And when you have gone someone will say, "Oh him. I thought he was still around. I used to see him often, only, all this time, I thought he was someone else."

THE FIRST DAY OF SPRING

When one is young everyday (as I remember it) is the first day of spring, all headlong and heedless. But, it turns out that life really is short, and before you know it you are old and filled with sadness. Nothing to do now but watch the birds, scratch a few petroglyphs for someone to puzzle over years from now, to stay out of the way and leave the bulk of the wanton destruction to those who are younger. The human race will evolve or go extinct. So what? It happens all the time. You never see saber-toothed tigers anymore. I suppose I should be sorry about that, but to tell the truth I never liked them. All that screaming and prowling around outside the house at night—— who needs it?

AUTUMN LEAVES

"And you call yourself a poet!" she said, laughing,
walking toward me. It was a woman I recognized,
though I couldn't remember her name. "Here you
are on the most beautiful day of autumn.... You
should be writing a poem." "It's a difficult subject
to write about, the fall," I said. "Nevertheless,"
she said, "I saw you drinking in the day, the
pristine blue sky, the warm sunshine, the brilliant
leaves of the maples and birches rustled slightly
by the cool west wind which is the harbinger of
winter. I saw how you watched that maple leaf
fall. I saw how you picked it up and noted the
flame color, touched here and there with bits of
gold and green and tiny black spots. I'm sure
that you saw in that leaf all the glory and pathos,
the joy and heartache of life on earth and yet
you never touched pen to paper." "Actually," I
said, "most of what I write is simply made up,
not real at all." "So...?" she said.

THE KISS

When I was eleven or twelve years old I thought a lot about kissing girls. Since I had never kissed a girl, romantically, that is, I was unsure how to go about it. I tried to imagine grabbing a girl roughly, as sometimes happened in movies, turning her around and kissing her hard on the lips. ("She struggled a moment then succumbed to the power of his passionate kiss....") Betsy O'Reilly would have knocked me down. How much pressure did one apply, should the lips just touch, lightly? (And what about French kissing? I could not imagine....) What was the proper duration of a kiss? The movies of that day often ended with a long kiss, the couple embraced, the music rose, but then the image faded. After the kiss what happens? Do you just stand there sort of embarrassed, shuffling your feet? You'd have to say something, but what? "Thank you for the really swell kiss, Alexandra?" The logistics were formidable. I thought about kissing a lot but I began to see that it was impossible.

FISHERMAN: STONEY POINT

Here's an old guy talking to himself. He reels in his bait and says, "Son, you've got to go out there again. I know how difficult it is; the rocks are treacherous, the water is deep. The winds can come up suddenly and there's no more than the thinnest line ties you to me. This is the way your life is going to be, out and back, again and again, partly in this world, partly in the other, never at home in either. Still, it's what you were born to do. You are young and strong, all steel and hooks. You know I'll do everything I can to bring you back safely. Go out there boy, and bring home a big fish for your old father to eat."

THE BACK COUNTRY

When you are in town wearing some kind of uniform is helpful, policeman, priest, etc. Driving a tank is very impressive, or a car with official lettering on the side. If that isn't to your taste you could join the revolution, wear an armband, carry a homemade flag tied to a broom handle, or a placard bearing an incendiary slogan. At the very least you should wear a suit and carry a briefcase and a cell phone, or wear a team jacket and a baseball cap and carry a cell phone. If you go into the woods, the backcountry, someplace past all human habitation, it is a good idea to wear orange and carry a rifle, or, depending on the season, carry a fishing pole, or a camera with a big lens. Otherwise it might appear that you have no idea what you are doing, that you are merely wandering the earth, no particular reason for being here, no particular place to go.

OVERBOARD

A piece of folded paper comes flying down from the deck above, over the stern of the ferryboat, and I feel the split-second shock of something irretrievably lost. Well, it isn't a child overboard. It isn't even the Magna Carta, pitched into the deep. Perhaps it's an old love letter, written in a loopy hand with little hearts dotting the i's, thrown ceremoniously by someone at the end of a marriage or an affair. Maybe it is a suicide note, tossed by someone who has reconsidered. Maybe it's the plans for a failed invention, or the first page of a bad novel. Most likely there's just some dope up above dumping garbage, a shopping list, or nothing, a blank piece of paper. It is just something that happened, anything, made memorable only by circumstance. The paper lingers there in the flat water at the center of the boat's wake and then, before you know it, is ten years past, a tiny speck. And then it's gone.

THE SNOWMAN MONOLOGUES

I don't have the top hat like my ancestors—well, my predecessors—had. I've got one of these little snap-brim caps like English motorists and golfers wear, and a very nice scarf. Quite bon vivant, I think. I've had to give up the pipe and I never drink. Still, I've got a big smile for everyone. I'm a traditionalist. I like the old songs, "White Christmas," "Ain't Misbehavin'," "Don't Get Around Much Anymore," songs like that. But I try to stay up to date, try to be aware of current events. I'm very concerned about global warming, for instance, but it's difficult in my field to get any real information. And what can I do? But I'm not complaining. I feel very much at home here, very much a part of my environment. It does get lonely at times though, there are so very few women in these parts, and I'm not the best looking guy around, with my strange build, black teeth and very odd nose. Sometimes I think they put my nose in the wrong place. Still, I have always hoped that someone would come along, someone who would melt in my arms. I think there must be a woman made for me, a snowwoman with whom I could become one. You wouldn't guess it to look at me but I'm a romantic. But it's getting rather late in the season for me. So, I'm inclined just to drift…. I don't have any problems getting through the night; it's the days that are so long and difficult now that spring is coming. Oh, spring is beautiful with the new buds on the trees and the bright sunshine, but it's such a melancholy season. It causes one to reflect…. Oh, but here I go, running off at the mouth again.

THE WRITER'S LIFE

I once believed that behind all the things I did—or more often, failed to do—there was a purpose, or at least some coherent principle, a raison d'être. If there is such a principle it has never become quite clear to me. Instead, over the years, I have managed to take a random selection of bad habits and herd them together into a life. Also, in order to disguise my absolute laziness I have mastered the age-old art of appearing to be productive when, actually, this is the only thing I'm doing. (Republicans suspected as much all along.) When someone comes up to my desk I get busy scribbling, totally preoccupied. "What? Oh, I'm sorry...." In my haste to appear industrious I find I have written "...and herd them together into a wife."

SUNDAY MORNING

I remember Sunday mornings in church when I was a child, then dinner at Aunt Pearl's house. The endless afternoon in the backyard with only her arthritic Pekinese for company, while inside the adults talked on and on about people who were dead. Think of learning the multiplication tables, true love, and the hours spent sitting on the edge of the bed in shorts and a t-shirt biting fingernails. I learned to smoke and to drive a car, how to cook spaghetti. Maybe all of that counts for something, and maybe someone, somewhere has been keeping score. Something like Social Security. Maybe one day I'll be given some sort of compensation (with certain deductions and penalties, no doubt) for accumulated life experience. Enough, perhaps, for a double-wide modular home on some rather low ground in an outlying district of what may not be heaven, but could certainly be a lot worse.

A WALK IN THE WOODS

Out here in the woods I can say anything I like without fear of contradiction. I am not faced with solving any of the great problems. I have only to cross a twenty-acre patch of mixed hardwoods and spruce, from one road to another without getting lost. Really, I am as free as the birds that flit from tree to tree, like the nuthatch or the white-throated sparrow, singing "old Sam Peabody, Peabody, Peabody." Here the trees are doing their usual dance—arms extended, fingertips raised, feet firmly planted, swaying from side to side. Just across the clearing there's a group of slender aspen, all in their spring party dresses, chattering away. Now the music begins again. "Moon River." Ladies choice. That tall homely one bends over to whisper to her friend and... oh, hell, they're all looking straight at me.

THE CLOUDS

The clouds sweep toward the western horizon as if they were nomads. Horses, men, children, dogs and goats and wives, cookpots and knives, banners and feathers, flags, ribbons, and hides, skulls borne on tall poles, all caught up in the whirl, the ecstasy of motion. They set off with a will, as if inspired. It is as if they served the great Kahn himself, a man of such presence that simply to behold his majesty would remove any doubt. To hear him speak banishes all hesitation. It is their manifest destiny! "Onward!" They would follow him across continents, across oceans if necessary…. But the thoughtless clouds move only at the behest of the wind, who is no one at all.

SOME THINGS TO THINK ABOUT

How cold is it? Will you need to wear your long johns or will the heavy wool pants over your blue jeans be enough? Which socks? Which boots? Which jacket? Scarf? Do you need the choppers with wool liners or just gloves? How fast will you be moving? If you are skiing or, God forbid, going to the mall, will you be too warm? Which direction is the wind from? Is it better to walk into the wind on your way out and have it at your back on the return, or vise-versa? Do you have a choice? Will the car start? Do you have blankets, fire extinguisher, flares, window scraper, extra gasoline, gas-line antifreeze, starting fluid, lock deicer, windshield washer fluid, a shovel, fresh water, flashlight, matches, candy bars? Do you have enough Kleenex? Ask yourself what you have forgotten. Do not ask yourself why or how. Remember to take your car keys out of your pocket before you put on your gloves.

RETIREMENT

I've been thinking of retiring, of selling the poetry business and enjoying my twilight years. It's a prose poem business, so it's a niche market. Still, after thirty-six years, I must have assets worth well in excess of $500. Perhaps the new owner of the business will want to diversify, go into novels or theatre, maybe even movies, or perhaps merge into a school or a movement. It won't matter to me once I've retired. Maybe I'll do a little traveling, winter in the Southwest. Take up golf. Spend more time with the family. Maybe I'll just walk around and look at things with absolutely no compulsion to say anything at all about them.

IMAGINARY READER

If poetry is your life, then your life must be the poem, a life that exists only for the reader. And who is the reader for whom you write? The imaginary reader? Perhaps it's a beautiful woman who is so taken with the words that she reads late into the night, propped on one elbow, only a sheet covers the curve of her hip, slips away from her bare shoulder. The summer breeze from the window teases her dark hair. Her lips move, from time to time, ever so slightly as she repeats a phrase that seems especially moving…. But probably, the imaginary reader is even more vaguely described, like God. The reader reads. Nothing happens. Nothing changes. The night goes on. He is still reading. He yawns, rubs his eyes. Any moment now the book will slip from his hands, so you write faster.

PARK

You could think of it as a small park. Well, not exactly a park, a little space between two busy streets, a city beautification project, an afterthought of city planners, all nicely bricked, with a park bench and an old maple tree that predates any planning, nothing else. It's a space nobody uses, really. Nobody sits on the bench. The drunks throw empty wine bottles here, now and then. And occasionally a bird, a crow or a sparrow, lands on a bare branch of the tree, on its way elsewhere. You could think of the leaves that have fallen as all of your dreams and hopes that have fallen and blown away, now that it is November. But there is no park really, and no bare branch where a bird could land. There is only this empty space that you cherish and protect, where once your heart was.

MIDDLE AGES

We have come now to the middle ages, our own private Middle Ages. It is a time of poverty and ignorance, the king's knights trampling the fields, destroying the crops, the peasant's hovel on fire, the pigs loose in the cabbage patch. And from behind the monastery walls, comes the sound of mournful singing. It is an age of faith, I suppose…. So, what comes next? It seems to me that we must be going backwards. We long ago passed the Age of Enlightenment. It must be the Dark Ages yet to come. Already rooks have gathered in the oak tree and the long ships have hoisted their black sails to set forth on stormy seas that are the color of your eyes.

SUBLIMATION

In scientific terms, sublimation is the direct conversion, under certain pressure and temperature conditions, of a solid into a gas, bypassing the liquid state. That's why that patch of ice on the sidewalk gets a little smaller every day even though the temperature never gets above zero. Something similar happens whenever I deposit a check into my bank account. The funds never reach a liquid state. It's the same when, thirty years later, you visit the house you lived in as a child. It's much smaller than you remember. People are older and smaller. Everyone notices when something dramatic happens—a car crash, a tree falling over. Yet the subtle process of the sublime goes on continually, without much notice. Whatever was continues to be, in the form of molecules or atoms or something, no more available now than it was back then.

A SENSE OF DIRECTION

I hope no one reads anything I've written with the expectation of finding any meaning or direction. I have no sense of direction whatsoever. Yet occasionally, as I walk along in my private fog, someone will stop (probably saying to himself "Here's guy who's obviously been around here for a hundred years,") and ask how to get from wherever we are, to say, the Mariner Mall or the Club Saratoga. So I oblige this person with detailed instructions accompanied by elaborate gestures, pointing, and maps drawn in the air. We part mutually gratified, each feeling a sense of accomplishment. Later I realize that my account had fatal flaws, and I imagine the lost soul saying, "What an idiot!" or "What a liar."

Nevertheless, there are a lot of books out there, and a few of them actually contain accurate information. But these books all have the same limitation: they were written for the living. One is only alive for a short while and dead for a very long time. Yet, as far as I know, no one has written anything that's of any use to the dead.

APPLE DOLLS

To look at their faces you'd think they remembered childhoods of summer, long hours at the old swimmin' hole, hayrides, blueberry pie, the county fair, kisses stolen under a sky full of stars. You'd think those wrinkles came from many years of hard work, sun and wind: the men in the fields, the women cooking, washing clothes, raising a dozen kids. But as they were born old, in their clean overalls and gingham dresses, they are perfect rubes, literally born yesterday. They don't even remember last week's bingo game or Tuesday's "Meals on Wheels" lunch, and indeed, that may be the reason for all this rosy-cheeked merriment.

EXPANDING UNIVERSE

Not just the galaxies, everything is moving farther apart. That's why when I reached out for that glass it fell and shattered after a long, long fall to the floor. That is why I missed the first step going upstairs. And I so rarely see my friends anymore, seldom see them rise above the horizon: a distant glimmer in the darkening firmament. And you and I, are we moving apart as well? I smile and wink, wave to you there on the far side of the bed.

HITCHHIKER

I pick up thistles and burdock, seeds of all sorts, on my pants legs as I walk the fields and ditches. Somewhere, way down the road, some will fall on fertile ground and begin the haphazard garden all over again. I pick up pebbles in my shoe treads and when they fall out they spawn streambeds, glacial moraines, mountain ranges. One day there will be a huge boulder right where your house is now, but it will take awhile.

AN ILL WIND: PARK POINT

Today there's a cold northeast wind blowing, Ice has piled up all along the water's edge like piles of broken glass giving off a strange blue light. Park Point is deserted, no one for five miles down the beach. Just the way I like it. The sand is frozen, mostly, so the walking is easy as I pick my way through the wrack and drift. Today I don't even leave footprints. Wind, sand, sun and water, a simplicity that defies comprehension, the barest essentials for the imagination's work. This shore has been pretty much the same for ten thousand years. Countless others have been here before me, musing and pondering, as they walked down the beach and disappeared forever. So here's what I'm thinking: wouldn't it be great if one of them dropped a big roll of hundred dollar bills and I found it?

HALDEMAN & ERLICHMAN

Very few people remember Haldeman & Erlichman, and even fewer know which is which. Which goes to show that even infamy is fleeting. "Haldeman & Erlichman," people say, "Haldeman & Erlichman. One of them is dead. I'm sure of that. Maybe both of them are dead." Haldeman & Erlichman, one of the lesser known of those comedy teams that include Burns & Allen, Abbott & Costello, Hamilton & Burr. Haldeman & Erlichman still play Republican fundraisers in places like Keokuk or Kokomo. They appear at Henry Kissinger's annual birthday party. They sing, they do magic tricks. "Hi! I'm Haldeman!" "I'm Erlichman! One of us has a crew cut." "Can you guess which one?"

WRONG TURN

You missed your turn two miles back because you weren't paying attention: daydreaming. So now you have decided to turn here, on the wrong road, just because you are too lazy to turn around. You have decided to turn here just because of some vague notion. You have decided to turn here just because you aren't smart enough not to. You have decided to turn here... just because. Listen, help is available. There are people who have experience with this kind of thing, people who have been through this. There are hotlines. There are brochures. There are programs, support groups. There is financial aid. Listen. The angels gather around you like gnats, strumming their guitars, singing songs of salvation, singing songs of freedom and diversity. But you aren't listening. Here you are on the genuine road less traveled. The road never snowplowed. Nothing to do but follow the ruts. Here the snow is too deep to turn around. You are going to have to follow this road to whatever nowhere it leads to.

THE TALK

He liked her immediately, her blue eyes, the way she looked at him as she listened, as if what he said was fascinating, the easy, natural way she laughed at all his jokes. Her rather conventional good looks and dress belied her intelligence. They had things in common, an interest in art and humanism, and they shared political views. She talked about the problems of coffee growers in Central America. He listened but he also thought about kissing her on the neck, there where her blond hair curled just behind her ear. He thought about other things, too. Mostly they laughed. Then she was silent. She looked at him. He saw that her eyes were gray, not blue. She was serious. She said, "Matt, this has gone too far in too short a time. I feel as though I'm being smothered. I have no time to myself anymore. I feel like you are always there. And I can't even so much as speak to another man." "What are you talking about?" he said, "We only met an hour ago!" "That is exactly what I'm trying to say," she said.

CULINARY CONSIDERATIONS

Lyle can't eat any onions or garlic. Phil is allergic to shellfish. Steve has a violent reaction to celery. Patricia is allergic to beef. Connie cannot eat processed meat. No fat for Joe. Dennis cannot eat any spicy food. Frank believes he is allergic to vinegar. Georganne is unable to tolerate mayonnaise. Michael is allergic to eggs and certain fish. Charlie and Sue do not eat meat, except fish. Thomas will eat no vegetables and no fish.... "Ick!" Dylan eats no meat or dairy products, except once when he ate an entire large cheese pizza. Peter will not eat cheese. Richard won't eat anything. Almost no one drinks anymore except Walt, who drinks too much and has to be sent home in a taxi. Elaine cannot stand Caroline so they have to be seated at opposite ends of the table.

HEREDITY

I have come to recognize certain genetic traits that I have inherited, patterns of behavior, certain involuntary actions. I can feel them happening—that worried look of my mother's, that almost angry, I-deserve-better-than-this look. And my father's manner of clearing his throat, the sleeves of his work shirt rolled to the elbow, a pencil poised motionless above a scrap of paper lying on the yellow oilcloth that covers the table, next to the white porcelain salt and pepper shakers with the red metal tops. Which means it must be sometime in the 1940s, the war still going on. Neither of them saying a word, as if stunned there in the dim late-night light of the kitchen. And what am I doing here? I should have been in bed hours ago.

REMEMBER

I'm trying to take up less space. I'm trying to remember to pick up after myself, to remember to take off my muddy boots before I come into the house. It's difficult. Partly because one branch of my family can trace their lineage directly back to an extinct species of water buffalo. I have to learn to talk quietly. To eat slowly, keeping my mouth closed. To wash and dry my little bowl and spoon and put them away. Turn off the lights, close the door softly. Descend the stairs carefully, avoiding the step that creaks, so not to wake the dead that are sleeping shoulder to shoulder. Those so long dead that their names and dates have eroded from their tombstones. The dead that can turn over in their narrow graves without ever touching the body next to them.

STEADY OR SLOWLY FALLING

Around this time every year the gloom swallows up someone unexpectedly, at random, it seems. We try to find reasons: He was depressed. He ate too much sugar. It seems hopeless, trying to figure things out. And yet, someone figured out the lever and the inclined plane. Someone invented glue and sandpaper, and someone learned which mushrooms were good to eat. Thank god it wasn't all left to you, you can't even boil water. But there's no use whining that your parents didn't leave you proper instructions or adequate tools, you simply have to make do. A stick to dig roots and grubs for the soup, and you have learned, by now, that it takes only a light tap with the same stick to put the baby down for his nap. Now, with the snow falling outside, the soup bubbling in the pot, the baby sleeping soundly in his crib, there's time for a moment of reflection.... Then the phone rings, and the baby starts crying just as the pot on the stove boils over, and, between one thing and another, your feet get tangled in the phone line. Which is a length of string tied to a couple of tin cans.

THE CHAIR

The chair has four legs but is a whole lot slower moving than, for instance, the ostrich, which has only two. Sometimes the chair does not move for weeks, even months at a time. Despite this sedentary almost catatonic lifestyle, it could be argued that the chair is every bit as intelligent as the ostrich, whose brain is smaller than its eye. And the chair is far less dangerous and unpredictable than the ostrich. The chair is more thoroughly domesticated. But it isn't a lazy boy. Don't slouch, don't lean back too far or the chair will throw you, for sure. The chair invites you to relax but to remain upright and attentive. The chair invites you to come to the table, sit down and eat your big bowl of ostrich stew.

THE CANADIAN WILDERNESS

I was awakened during the night by something inside my sleeping bag rubbing against my back near my shoulder blade, scratching me. I reached around and it felt like one of those stiff cloth labels, the kind they attach to pillows and mattresses and such, the ones that say DO NOT REMOVE UNDER PENALTY OF LAW. I grabbed hold and gave it a yank and much to my shock found that it was attached to my back! I lay there a few moments, my mind racing, my back still in pain where I'd pulled at the label. I tried to calm down. I must have been dreaming. I felt again, carefully. It was definitely attached to my back. I didn't know what to do. Should I wake the others, say, "I've got a mattress label attached to my back!" What could they do, anyway? It isn't really a medical emergency and we're camped deep in the Canadian wilderness, no roads, a hundred miles from the nearest settlement, and no phone reception. Outside the tent the sky is clear, a nearly full moon shining over the lake, no sound except for a little breeze in the spruce trees. It's beautiful, nowhere to go, nothing to be done.

CONJURER

After years of practice you are able to produce the illusion of a human figure: a man, perhaps. A man wearing a navy blue suit, a middle-aged, more-or-less law-abiding citizen. The finer points, however, still elude you. For one thing, you've gotten the ears too large, the hair is unruly, unkempt looking, and the sleeves of his jacket and the legs of his pants are too long, or else his arms and legs are too short. The brown shoes are on the wrong feet. No matter how you try the figure isn't quite right. On the other hand, fog and trees are fairly easy to conjure up and help to mask the errors. The droplets of water weighing down the delicate needles of the tall pines gives the scene a sort of oriental look, a kind of ancient dignity. And it gives the figure a rather contemplative aspect, the monk alone in the wilderness. But now the suit looks out of place…. Passersby will say, "Did you see that goofy looking guy over there in the trees?" "Goofy, yes…but very well dressed."

GOINGS ON AROUND THE HOUSE

There's a spider crawling up the wall towards the crown molding and I don't like the looks of him. I know you can learn by watching spiders. I know about Robert the Bruce and Whitman's noiseless, patient spider. But maybe Whitman's hearing wasn't all that good, maybe that spider was going about his work whistling, a kind of annoying, tuneless whistle. Whitman said he could go and live with the animals, and people do. Generally, though, we tend to be rather choosy about which animals. People often want a certain breed of animal, a Jack Russell Terrier or a Siamese cat, nothing else will do. Of course, there are people who live with rats and snakes, and god knows what else. I don't care. There is a spider on my ceiling and I don't like him.

THE STATE OF THE ECONOMY

There might be some change on top of the dresser at the back, and there are some pennies in a jar in the closet. We should check the washer and the dryer. Check under the floor mats of the car. The couch cushions. I have some books and CDs I could sell, and there are a couple of big bags of aluminum cans in the basement. Only trouble is that there isn't enough gas in the car to get around the block. And the price of gasoline goes up every day. I'm expecting a check sometime next week, which, if we are careful, will get us through to payday. In the meantime with your one-dollar rebate check and a few coins we have enough to walk to the store and buy a quart of milk and a newspaper. On second thought, forget the newspaper.

MOCKINGBIRD

I remember when I was a child I had a pair of canaries in a cage in my bedroom. I had the idea that I would raise and sell canaries. I asked one of my sisters if she remembered them. She remembered that they were parakeets, not canaries. I asked another sister. She said she didn't remember any canaries but she remembered how mean I was to her. My youngest sister doesn't remember having birds but thinks that we had a pet rabbit. I don't remember that. My brother thinks we had a pet crow that talked. I don't remember a crow but I remember we had a myna bird for a while that said, "Hello sweetiepie" but he belonged to someone else. My mother says that she would never have allowed birds or any other animals in the house. I remember how the female canary ignored the male but chirped plaintively to a mockingbird that sang outside my window all summer long.

BLUE MOON

The moon looks worried, rising above Lake Superior. The moon looks so unhappy, so pale. The moon has not been well. The moon has had a lot of problems with meteors, especially in youth. And night after night the moon watches the same old earth rise.... It hasn't been easy for the moon. The moon.... The moon.... The moon this and the moon that. You drive faster but the moon keeps pace, looking sadly into your car window. "Why are you leaving," the moon wonders, "and where will you go?"

INDEX OF TITLES